A *WESTERN HORSEMAN* BOOK

THE
WESTERN HORSEMAN
RECIPE FILE

Cowboy-Style Cooking at its Best

Edited By Fran Devereux Smith

LOGO ART: RON BONGE

THE *WESTERN HORSEMAN*®
RECIPE FILE

Published by
WESTERN HORSEMAN® magazine
2112 Montgomery St.
Fort Worth, TX 76107
817-737-6397

www.westernhorseman.com

Design, Typography, and Production
Sandy Cochran Graphic Design
Fort Collins, Colorado

Front and Back Cover Photos by
Jennifer Denison

Printing
Versa Press, Inc.
East Peoria, Illinios

Made in the United States of America

First Printing: February 2015

ISBN 978-1-4930-0179-8

ACKNOWLEDGMENTS

You might know this type of food as campfire cooking, bunkhouse chow, a ranch-wife recipe, rodeo-road food or Dutch-oven specialty. You might have eaten such food at a spring branding, old-timers' reunion, church social, fairgrounds arena or chuck-wagon cook-off. No matter by what name the food is known or where it is served, the meal is an Old West legacy that has made it's way naturally into the 21st century. Here at *Western Horseman*, we simply call it cowboy-style cooking.

Such cooking has become an American tradition celebrated by city dwellers and rural folk alike, and appreciated by the ranchers and the cowboys who once did and sometimes still do ride out with the wagon. Today, many of the genre's recipes can make smooth transitions from Dutch oven and campfire to microwave and food processor, even to modern healthy-eating concepts. But the flavor of the Old West remains.

All of us here at *Western Horseman* tip our hats to all of you who have been a part of preserving cowboy-style cooking through the years. From our outfit to yours, thanks for honoring a tradition of the great American West.

CONTENTS

INTRODUCTION

The soft whistle of a lantern being lit and its flickering golden flame are often the first signs of morning on a wagon parked in a Texas pasture. The cook quietly mills around the camp a few hours before dawn, using the glow of lantern and moonlight to gather the supplies and cast-iron skillets he needs to get breakfast going for a crew of hungry cowboys. More than 1,200 miles to the north in southern Montana, a ranch wife in her bathrobe and slippers wanders into the kitchen, flips on the light and also starts collecting everything she needs to make the morning meal.

Sitting down and sharing a meal or a "square," as it's sometimes called on ranches, is as much a part of cowboy values and the Western lifestyle as a top hand saddling his or her own horse and making sure the critters have been fed before sitting down to eat. A savvy cowboss makes sure to hire the best cook around during roundups and brandings because a crew works hard when they are happy and their bellies are full. The ranch wife mentioned above says that she feels privileged to cook for a cowboy crew because a good meal is something they look forward to each day, and for some of the young men sitting down at the table for breakfast, it's the closest thing they have to a home and family environment.

Hearing these things has inspired my interest in chuck-wagon cooking and the evolution of contemporary cowboy cuisine. Like most horse and ranch folks, I don't consider myself a bona fide "foodie," and definitely not a gourmet chef. However, growing up in a small town with few restaurants and with parents who worked full-time jobs, I learned to cook simple suppers at a young age. I also packed slow-cookers filled with barbecued beef and sloppy Joe, and casserole dishes of creamed corn and baked beans to the branding corrals or church potlucks. But I always wanted to cook for a crew, and I finally got a taste of that when I signed up for Kent Rollins' chuck-wagon cooking school and reported on it in the February 2012 issue of *Western Horseman*.

Western Horseman is rooted in the stock-horse industry. A unique lifestyle surrounds those who own and ride horses or ranch for a living, and food is a definite part of it, from the family sitting down at the dinner table to preparing a meal for a branding-day gathering to packing a snack for the trail.

Through the years, the magazine always has included recipes for these and other occasions. The most noted contributor was the late Stella Hughes, a writer and ranch wife from Arizona. For much of the last half of the past century, Stella contributed regularly to *Western Horseman*. Her focus, typically ranch-related, often targeted the food that fueled the cowboys. Filled with good humor and a savvy understanding of human nature, Stella's articles rang true with readers, who also successfully reproduced her tasty fare for their own outfits. Ultimately her "Bacon & Beans" column, which ran through 2000, showcased Stella's knack for serving up recipes alongside witty stories and lessons learned while living on the remote reservation ranch that her husband, Mack, managed for 30 years. Those recipes were compiled into *Western Horseman*'s cookbook *Bacon & Beans,* which was released in 1990 and has become a staple on the shelf in many ranch kitchens.

In 2007, when the magazine underwent a landmark redesign, the staff dedicated a page in the magazine to cowboy cuisine. Many of the featured recipes have been old family favorites that I revived and photographed in my kitchen. Some recipes were submitted by readers, and other recipes have been collaborations with award-winning chuck-wagon cooks, including Jean Cates, Sue Cunningham, Tom Perini, Kent Rollins and Grady Spears, whose recipes are included in this cookbook.

The magazine also held a recipe contest, with the winner receiving an all-expenses paid trip to Abilene, Texas, to attend the Western Heritage Classic, an annual event held each May that includes the Ranch Horse Association of America National Finals, a ranch rodeo, entertainment, match horse racing and a chuck-wagon cooking contest. *Western Horseman* received more than a thousand entries, but Bob Heavirland, a chuck-wagon cook from North Branch, Minn., became the winner with his recipe for Drunken Roast Beef, which appears in this book as adapted from a recipe often prepared by the Circle F outfit in Texas.

I had the opportunity to meet Bob and his wife, Vicki, during their trip and joined them for lunch at Perini Ranch Steakhouse in Buffalo, Texas. With Tom and Lisa Perini as our hosts, we feasted on such specialties as quail legs, dry-rubbed ribs, jalapeno bites, green chile hominy, Zucchini Perini, grilled ribeye and bread pudding with whiskey sauce.

Feedback on the magazine's recipe page had been favorable, but in 2012 we started thinking of ways to make the column even better and create our own "celebrity" cowboy chef. Interest in chuck-wagon and Dutch-oven cooking was growing in mainstream audiences, fueled by exposure on the Food Network. Thanks to an episode of *Throwdown with Bobby Flay* that ran in the fall of 2010, we learned about a chuck-wagon cook then living in Byers, Texas, Kent Rollins. He had been challenged by Flay to see who could cook the best chicken-fried steak. Rollins won the throwdown, but most appealing to us were his authenticity, favorable reputation on ranches, quick wit and storytelling abilities.

To see what this character was about, I attended his cooking school and came away with the best person since Stella to write the magazine's recipe column. For two years, Rollins has shared his recipes and stories in the magazine. During that time, he has made more appearances on the Food Network, including two rounds of heated competition on the show *Chopped*, where he finished second both times. His cowboy cooking, good values and heart of gold have stolen the hearts of amateur foodies, and he has made cowboy cuisine cool.

This book is the first cookbook that *Western Horseman* has published since *Bacon & Beans*. We've wrangled some of recipes that have appeared in the magazine since 2007. Some are from Rollins, Hughes and other cowboy cooks, and staff and friends of the magazine have submitted the rest. These recipes are a blend of old-fashioned favorites that have been handed down for generations, as well as new twists on traditional dishes. Taste and appearance, of course, have been considerations, as well as regional diversity and ease of preparation, but also important is that recipe ingredients are staples in most pantries so there are no unplanned trips to the grocery. Many of the recipes can be prepared in Dutch ovens and cooked outside over the coals or in the comfort of your kitchen. Altogether, these recipes represent the many flavors of the Western lifestyle.

The cowboy way of life is still alive in the West, but it has changed. Trucks, trailers and four-wheelers are primary methods of transportation. Few ranches roll out the wagon anymore and most cook shacks

Each fall, Jennifer Denison hosts a Harvest Party at her Colorado home and cooks some of the spread over the fire

CINDY VALADE

have closed. However, that doesn't mean there aren't plenty of hard-working, hungry cowboys and cowgirls who love to eat still out there in the West or points beyond, where enthusiastic horsemen and –women love the lifestyle. This cookbook is for them and their families. We hope the recipes offer inspiration for creative cooking, and that the food unites your family and crew around the dinner table for many memorable meals.

Jennifer Denison
Senior Editor
Western Horseman

APPETIZERS AND SNACKS 1

When you think about cowboys and cooking, images of chuck wagons on the great cattle drives from 1866 to 1886, and cowboys gathered around a campfire for a meal come to mind. Legendary trail drover and Texas cattleman Charles Goodnight is credited for developing the chuck wagon, one of the most iconic symbols of the West, during a cattle drive with Oliver Loving in 1866. Goodnight mounted a military chuck box on an Army wagon, creating a mobile kitchen that became a model for other cattle drovers and wagon manufacturers. As these wagons rolled across the range, they quickly became the heart of the roundups, a home for roaming cowboys, and storage for provisions, bedrolls, firearms and other essential gear.

The chuck-wagon cook, sometimes referred to as the "cookie" or "coosie," was hired for a wage considerably higher than the cowboys, and rightly so. A savvy trail boss knew a hungry crew wasn't a happy crew. Second-in-command on the trail, the cookie did far more than set up camp, prepare meals and keep the coffee boiling. He also served as a doctor, dentist, mechanic, repairman, farrier or seamstress, and filled any other role as needed.

One thing the cookie didn't do, however, was serve hors d'oeuvres before a meal. The only appetizer an early cowboy might have carried would have been some jerky or hard biscuits. Nowadays, only a few wagons still run on ranches, and cowboys often stuff jerky, granola bars and trail mix in their saddlebags for snacks to get them through the day.

In this chapter, you find recipes for these and other simple yet satisfying snacks, plus hearty appetizers that can curb a crew's hunger until the dinner bell rings. Appetizers set the stage for a sit-down meal with family or a dinner party with neighbors. The best appetizers are small and easy to eat with one hand, so you can mingle while you munch. Pair crackers or chips with any of the salsa or dip recipes on the following pages to take the edge off anyone's hunger pangs. For an appetizer that could be considered cowboy cuisine, try the recipes for warm artichoke hearts or bruschetta topped with cream cheese, tomatoes, garlic, basil and olive oil. Make pastry puffs stuffed with sausage or cheese ahead of time and freeze. Then when company comes calling, pop the snacks in the oven and they'll be ready to serve in minutes.

Once the cookie made camp, the chuck-box covering typically dropped down to stand on hinged supports and serve as a kitchen counter.

JENNIFER DENISON

Guacamole on the Range

*This is great on top of the Quick Quesadillas included in this chapter
or as a dip for tortilla chips.*

2 peeled garlic cloves

3 large avocados

½ teaspoon salt

½ teaspoon chili powder

2 teaspoons lemon juice

½ cup finely chopped white onion

½ teaspoon black pepper

3 drops Tabasco®

2 cups chopped Roma tomatoes

cilantro for garnish

Rub a wooden bowl with garlic cloves. Peel the avocados and cut into small chunks.
Set pit aside for use later.

Gently mix the avocado, salt, chili powder, lemon juice, onion, black pepper and Tabasco® in the
garlic-rubbed bowl, without smashing the avocado chunks. Place the avocado pit in the center
of the mixture to prevent the guacamole from turning brown.

Refrigerate until 10 minutes before serving. Gently fold in Roma tomatoes. Garnish with cilantro,
and serve with tortilla chips or add a dollop on top of your quesadilla.

Editor's note: Although this recipe doesn't say to remove the avocado pit from the dish before serving,
some cooks do just that. Other cooks prefer leaving the pit in an avocado-based dish to help maintain
freshness and prevent discoloration.

Jeff Tracy
Oregon City, Oregon

Tomato-Less Salsa

*Not that there's anything wrong with tomatoes, but this salsa doesn't need 'em.
Addictive with tortilla chips. You can make a meal of it.*

1 16-ounce can black beans, rinsed and drained

1 16-ounce can sweet corn kernels, rinsed and drained

½ cup cilantro, finely chopped

½ red onion, finely chopped

2 garlic cloves, minced or put through garlic press

Rinse corn and black beans and drain in colander. Place in mixing bowl.
Stir in all other ingredients and serve.

Cynthia McFarland
Williston, Florida

All-Around Mix

More than a traditional dip, this versatile recipe can season soup,
serve as a salad and add festive color to any table.

2 cans black beans, rinsed and drained

1 can pinto or Ranch-Style beans, rinsed and drained

1 can black-eyed peas, rinsed and drained

1 can sweet yellow corn, drained

2 cans shoe-peg corn, drained

2 cans original Ro*Tel® Tomatoes or Ro*Tel® with lime and cilantro, drained

1 to 3 fresh jalapeños, depending on your taste, deseeded and chopped

3 to 4 Roma tomatoes, chopped

1 onion, chopped, variety of preference

3 to 4 avocados, cubed, with seeds to help maintain freshness

garlic, sea salt, pepper and chopped fresh cilantro to taste

1 lime

Combine all ingredients except avocado in large bowl and mix well. Add avocado with seeds, which help keep it fresh-looking, last or serve separately on the side. Squeeze juice of one lime over mix in bowl and stir again. Serve with Fritos® Scoops® for dipping.

Tip: This All-Around Mix is a great stand-alone salad and also makes the perfect topping for tacos or any Mexican-style dish. Prefer soup? Just omit the avocado and add the mix to the pot for substance and wonderful flavor. The mix works well with cut-up chicken in chicken broth as a soup base or with hamburger in beef broth, and the soup freezes well.

Tonya Ward
Weatherford, Texas

Colorado cowgirl Kim Simshauser, at left, and Texas horsewoman Tonya Ward have worked with Western Horseman *sales reps and magazine advertisers for a number of years.*

JENNIFER DENISON

JENNIFER DENISON

Ranch Sausage Stars

This summer, when the moon is bright, pass around a plate of these tasty bites perfect for a casual get-together with friends.

1 pound pork sausage, crumbled, browned and drained well of grease
3 cups shredded cheddar cheese
1 cup ranch salad dressing
1 can, or 2¼ ounces, ripe olives, sliced or chopped
½ cup chopped red bell pepper
1 package of small wonton wrappers

Preheat oven to 350 degrees.

Blot browned sausage dry with paper towels, then combine with cheese, salad dressing, olives and red bell pepper. Set aside.

Press one wonton wrapper into each cup on a muffin tin, shaping wrapper into a star shape by pinching in the middle of all four sides. Bake 5 minutes. Be careful not to overbake, as the corners of the wonton wrappers burn easily.

Remove wrappers from muffin tin, place on baking sheet, and fill with sausage mixture. Bake 5 minutes or until bubbly. Yields 50 servings.

Tip: I like the marble cheddar, or you can use a mixture of cheddar and Monterey Jack. If desired, you can freeze the sausage mixture and the shaped and prebaked wrappers in separate containers. Ziploc® bags also work great. Just thaw, fill the wrappers and bake on the day you wish to serve them.

Linda Knowles
Fort Worth, Texas

From the *American Paint Horse Foundation Cookbook*, 2006.

JENNIFER DENISON

Chicken Fiesta Dip

This warm, hearty dip can spice up Sunday supper or a Super Bowl party.

1 8-ounce brick of cream cheese, softened
1 ½ cups Mexican cheese, shredded
1 4-ounce can green chilies, undrained
1 envelope taco seasoning
1 teaspoon garlic
½ teaspoon hot sauce
½ cup Ro*Tel® tomatoes
6 ounces cooked chicken, finely chopped or shredded

Preheat oven to 350 degrees.

Over low heat, mix cream cheese, 1 cup of Mexican cheese, green chilies, seasonings and the tomatoes. Stir in chicken. Spread mixture into a casserole dish.

Bake at 350 degrees for 20 minutes or until warm. Sprinkle with remaining cheese and let stand 10 minutes. Serve with tortilla chips.

Jennifer Denison
Sedalia, Colorado

Jalapeño-Glazed Cheese Ball

Spice up your appetizer tray and add a bit of color to your holiday table.

2 cups sour cream
1 cup cheddar cheese
1 cup pecans, chopped
jalapeño jelly

Mix sour cream, cheese and pecans together well.

Mold mixture into desired shape and chill 1 hour.

Spread jalapeño jelly on top. Serve with crackers.

Marsha Witte
Peyton, Colorado

White Trash

You won't throw out this "trash," but you might give it away during the holidays.

3 pounds almond bark, typically two 1½-pound packages
4 cups Honeycomb cereal
6 cups pretzels
12 ounces mixed nuts
1 cup toasted pecans or dry-roasted peanuts

Mix dry ingredients in large pan or roaster. Set aside.

Melt almond bark in a heavy pan over low heat, or use microwave. If microwaving, start with 90 seconds at high, stir, and then heat for about 12 to 15 seconds at a time, stirring each time, until bark is melted.

Pour melted almond bark over mix in large pan and stir well to coat.

Spread white trash on foil-lined baking sheet or foil on countertop to cool and set.
When set, break the trash into small-to-medium pieces and store in airtight container.

Tip: The thinner the layer on the foil, the easier it is to break the white trash into pieces.
To set the trash more quickly, spread white trash on foil-lined cookie sheet and then
place it in the refrigerator or freezer for a short period of time until set.
White trash keeps well in fridge and freezes well.

Fran Devereux Smith
Fort Worth, Texas

Easy Beef Jerky

*Easy to make and easy to pack—and it's the perfect snack
when you're horseback all day or driving to the next rodeo.*

3-pound round roast,
    thinly sliced
¾ cup soy sauce
¾ cup Worcestershire
4 tablespoons ketchup
¾ teaspoon pepper
¾ teaspoon garlic powder
¾ teaspoon onion salt
1½ teaspoons salt
4 to 5 shakes Liquid Smoke

Ask your butcher to slice your roast
very thinly for your jerky.

Mix all other ingredients well and
pour over the sliced roast. Let the
meat marinate for at least 2 to 3 hours,
preferably overnight.

After the meat has marinated, place
single slices in the dehydrator for
7 hours.

Kami Peterson
Elizabeth, Colorado

*Kami Peterson, a senior account manager with the
Western Horseman sales department, also is an avid team roper.*

JENNIFER DENISON

JENNIFER DENISON

Chili-Cheese Squares

Fun and flavorful, these bite-sized squares can add spice and substance to your appetizer trays, go with breakfast, lunch and dinner, or stand alone as a hearty snack.

2 pounds cheddar cheese, grated
2 4-ounce cans chopped green chilies
12 eggs, beaten well
1 teaspoon garlic salt

Preheat oven to 350 degrees.

Layer the cheese and chilies in a buttered baking dish. Combine the beaten eggs with the garlic salt, and pour over the cheese.

Bake for 30 minutes, or until the eggs test done. Cool, and then cut into small squares.

Robert Boyd
Trent, Texas

Sausage Biscuits

Here's an appetizer that adds a bit of substance to the usual array of dips and chips.

1 pound sausage
8 ounces sharp cheese
3 cups baking mix

Preheat oven to 350 degrees.

Melt cheese in a pan. Add raw sausage and baking mix. Set aside to cool.

When mixture is cool, form into balls about the size of a walnut. Place in a shallow baking pan.
Bake at 350 degrees until browned and sausage is thoroughly cooked.

Patricia Wilson
Topeka, Kansas

Quick Quesadillas

*Friends coming to visit? You can create scrumptious quesadillas
in the time it takes to jingle the horses and saddle yours.*

2 pounds chorizo
2 pounds mild Italian sausage
2 pounds extra-sharp cheddar cheese
1 pound smoked Gouda
2 red bell peppers
2 green bell peppers
3 ounces dried pepper flakes
3 ounces minced garlic
freshly chopped cilantro to taste
24 large flour tortillas
extra-virgin olive oil
seasoning salt, optional

Preheat grill to low or medium temperature. Slice chorizo and Italian sausage into thin, diagonal slices.
Brown in a skillet, but don't overcook.

Grate both cheeses and place in separate bowls. Chop bell peppers and cilantro into small pieces.

Lightly baste a tortilla with olive oil. Sprinkle both cheeses on the tortilla until it's completely covered.
Add minced garlic, cooked sausage, bell peppers, pepper flakes and cilantro to taste on top of the cheese.
If desired, sprinkle seasoning salt on top of the vegetables.

Grill 6 to 8 minutes until cheese is melted.
Top with the Guacamole on the Range recipe in this chapter, if desired.

Jeff Tracy
Oregon City, Oregon

Cowboy Bistro Salsa

*A simple cowboy favorite, but one that's requested almost daily
when the Cowboy Bistro opens at a major rodeo.*

1 29-ounce can tomato sauce
1 bunch cilantro, leaves only, chopped
1½ teaspoons red pepper flakes
4 to 5 cloves garlic, finely minced

Mix all together well and let chill at least 1 hour for flavors to blend.

Linda and Ted Wiese
Payette, Idaho

The Cowboy Bistro, a mobile kitchen that feeds hungry contestants at major rodeos, is part of Ted and
Linda Wiese's Rockin W Rodeo Ministries, which serves both body and soul.

CORY WEISE

JENNIFER DENISON

Tortilla Wraps

These creamy tortilla wraps make great appetizers or simple snacks.

8 ounces softened cream cheese
1 teaspoon garlic powder
1 teaspoon dill weed
salt and pepper to taste
¼ cup finely chopped green bell pepper
¼ cup finely chopped red bell pepper
¼ cup finely chopped celery
¼ cup finely chopped seedless cucumber
1 grated carrot
2 finely chopped green onions
¼ cup chopped black and green olives
½ cup grated Mexican cheese
6 large flour tortillas

In large bowl, beat cream cheese, garlic powder, dill weed, salt and pepper with hand mixer.
Add remaining ingredients and mix well by hand. Put in freezer for 15 minutes,
then take out and mix well again by hand.

Warm tortillas and spread cream cheese mixture on a tortilla,
leaving a half-inch border around the edges. Roll tortilla tightly.
Repeat process with remaining tortillas.
Cover and refrigerate overnight.

Prior to serving, cut off ends of each roll and discard.
Use a knife to cut tortilla rolls into pinwheels about ½- to ¾-inch wide.

Robert Boyd
Trent, Texas

Fruit Salsa
and Cinnamon-Sugar Chips

Cinnamon-sugar tortilla chips are the perfect accomplices to aid and abet a fresh-fruit appetizer!

Fruit Salsa

diced fresh fruits
juice of one lime
1 tablespoon honey

Mix well. Serve with cinnamon-sugar tortilla chips described below.

Cinnamon-Sugar Tortilla Chips

flour tortillas, cut into squares
cooking oil
cinnamon
sugar

Preheat oven to 350 degrees.

Toss tortilla squares with oil and place in a single layer on a shallow baking pan.
Bake at 350 degrees until crisp.

Remove from oven. While still warm, sprinkle with cinnamon and sugar. Enjoy!

Patricia Wilson
Topeka, Kansas

Corn Dip

Make this company-worthy dip in advance to let the flavors blend. Little prep time required!

2 16-ounce packages of cream cheese
2 packages dry Hidden Valley® Ranch Dressing Mix
1 can chopped green chilies, drained and patted dry
1 small can chopped black olives
½ red pepper, chopped
1 can whole-kernel corn, drained and patted dry

Combine cream cheese and dressing mix together. Add remaining ingredients and mix well.
Refrigerate and let dip sit for a few hours for flavors to blend before serving.

Patricia Wilson
Topeka, Kansas

Haystacks

Anybody would love to have haystacks like these in the kitchen!

1 12-ounce package butterscotch chips
2 cans shoestring potatoes
1 cup peanuts
1 tablespoon peanut butter

Melt butterscotch chips in the microwave, stirring often.

Stir in peanut butter. Add shoestring potatoes and peanuts, and stir until coated.

Drop by tablespoonfuls, or to size desired, onto wax paper and let cool completely.

Susan Morrison
Fort Worth, Texas

Western Horseman *magazine's Managing Editor Susan Morrison also has written* Ride Smarter *with clinician Craig Cameron, his second book with the outfit.*

ROSS HECOX

Fiesta Cabbage Salsa

*After a hot day's work, cool off around the wagon with a fresh grazing recipe
that doesn't require building a fire.*

6 Roma tomatoes, cubed
1 purple onion, diced
¾ cup jalapeños from a jar, diced
¼ cup jalapeño juice from the jar
¼ cup lime juice
16-ounce bag coleslaw
1 to 1½ teaspoons garlic salt

Combine all ingredients in a large bowl. Cover and refrigerate at least 5 hours.
Serve with chips, tacos or any Mexican dish.

Tip: You can eat this immediately, but I think it's even better if you let it sit in the icebox overnight
and let the flavors mingle.

Kent Rollins
Hollis, Oklahoma

From *A Taste of Cowboy* by Kent Rollins, © 2015 by Kent Rollins.
Reprinted by permission of Houghton Mifflin Harcourt Publishing Company. All rights reserved.

ROSS HECOX

JENNIFER DENISON

Rodeo Road Bars

Make a batch of these hearty bars to take down the trail or on your next road trip.

4 cups oats
1½ cups oat flour or rice flour
2 cups shredded coconut
1 cup nuts or seeds
½ cup brown sugar
1 cup raisins or other dried fruit
¾ cup oil
1 cup brown rice syrup or corn syrup, warmed

Preheat oven to 325 degrees.

Mix first six ingredients well. Stir in oil and warm syrup, and mix well.
Spread mixture in a rimmed 9-by-13-inch baking sheet lined with foil.

Bake 1 hour or until browned. Cut into bars while still warm in pan. Let cool completely before
removing from pan. Best enjoyed with coffee on late-night drives to the next rodeo.

Kate Mote
Culver, Oregon

From *Bring 'Em on Home: A Collection of Recipes from Famous Rodeo Cowboys and Their Families*, by
Bonnie Beers and Kimber Beers. A portion of all cookbook sales is donated to the Justin Cowboy Crisis Fund.

25

Appetizing Artichokes

Serve these easy-to-make appetizers warm from the oven.
Guests will think you spent hours preparing for their visit.

1 14-ounce can of artichoke hearts, drained and chopped
1 cup real mayonnaise
1 cup, about 4 ounces, Parmesan cheese
1 clove garlic, minced
1 loaf French bread or baguettes, sliced

Preheat oven to 350 degrees.

Mix first four ingredients together. Spread mixture on bread slices or baguettes.

Bake for 20 minutes or until golden.

Nancy Hughes
Fort Worth, Texas

Bruschetta with a Twist

The cream cheese layer adds a twist to this traditional starter and keeps the baguette slices
crisp longer… not that you're going to have any leftovers to worry about!

1 baguette, French or Italian
olive oil cooking spray
8 ounces cream cheese, softened
1½ pounds, about 6 to 8, ripe plum tomatoes
2 to 4 garlic cloves, or more to taste, minced or put through garlic press
10 fresh basil leaves, snipped with scissors into thin "ribbons"
1 tablespoon olive oil
salt and freshly ground black pepper to taste

Heat oven to 450 degrees.

Cut baguette into slices, about ½-inch thick. You might need to bake in two batches if the loaf is large.
Lay slices on a baking sheet and spray tops with olive oil cooking spray.
Place baking sheet in oven on top rack and cook for about 5 minutes.
You want the slices just to start turning golden. Remove slices from oven and set aside to cool.

Chop plum tomatoes into small pieces. Place in colander until juice drains, then place tomatoes
in mixing bowl. Add garlic. Using clean scissors, snip basil leaves into ribbons over the bowl.
Stir in olive oil and mix all gently together. Add salt and pepper to taste.

To assemble, spread a thin layer of cream cheese on each toasted baguette slice.
Using a slotted spoon, place a heaping tablespoon or two of tomato mixture on top of the cream cheese.
Serve immediately and enjoy!

Cynthia McFarland
Williston, Florida

Big Loop Trail Mix

You won't go hungry with this snack in your pocket—even if you're horseback all day.

7½-ounce package sunflower kernels
7½-ounce package whole almonds
6-ounce package sliced almonds
12 ounces golden raisins and/or 12 ounces dark raisins, as you prefer
16-ounces dry-roasted peanuts or mixed nuts, as you prefer
8 ounces Reese's® Pieces and/or 8 ounces M&M'S®, as you prefer

Mix all ingredients thoroughly in a large bowl, then seal in an airtight container or bag. Throw the whole bag in the wagon when a group is on hand, or sack an individual portion for your saddlebags.

Tip: For one or two portions, a small, freezer-weight zip bag holds up better on the trail than a lightweight sandwich bag. This recipe has options to suit almost anyone's taste, and exact measurements have never been an issue. I've substituted many times through the years, depending on what was in the pantry or available at the store, and with no complaints. However, years ago my family expressed a preference for only golden raisins and Reese's Pieces.

Fran Devereux Smith
Fort Worth, Texas

Fran Smith, who worked on Western Horseman *magazine's editorial staff before becoming book-publishing director, has been with the outfit 20-plus years.*

ROSS HECOX

27

Kit Haddock, Monument, Colo., summons the crew to the wagon with a triangle-shaped dinner bell.
JENNIFER DENISON

Come and Get It!

You've probably seen the chuck-wagon cook or pioneer wife in old Western film ring the dinner bell and yell, "Come and get it!"

While somebody ringing the dinner bell was not always the case on a farm, ranch or wagon, it is common knowledge that ringing a bell is a call to gather people. Think about church bells or school bells.

Just like most pieces of cowboy equipment, the dinner bell originated out of necessity. Early farming, ranching and cowboy crews worked over vast spreads of land and were not always together.

According to the American Bell Association International, Inc., the practice of ringing a dinner bell became customary in the 19th and 20th centuries to summon the crews spread over long distances to come to headquarters or the chuck wagon for a meal. In the West, the most common dinner bell was a metal bar shaped like a triangle and hung from a piece of leather. The cook rang the bell by striking it with a short, straight metal bar, and sometimes shouted the familiar refrain, "Come and get it!"

—Jennifer Denison

SALADS   2

On the chuck wagon, the cookie didn't stock many fruits and vegetables, except potatoes, onions, peppers, peaches, and maybe some dried fruit for a cobbler. Most of the produce he used was grown locally, picked in the wild or obtained through trade. Today, ranch families still prefer to buy locally and naturally grown produce, or plant their own gardens to ensure their produce is free of harmful pesticides and as healthy as possible. Having gardens also saves these people the time and trouble of driving to town, which for some can be an all-day trip.

Salad isn't considered traditional cowboy or chuck-wagon fare, but during the warm summer months heavy comfort food isn't as appealing as a fresh fruit or vegetable salad, especially after a long day of working in the sun. The recipes here show you how to toss in some chicken, pasta, beans, a flavorful dressing or other ingredients to make a light, healthy meal.

One traditional chuck-wagon staple through the years has been chowchow, a pickled relish made from cabbage, tomatoes, peppers, onions and spices, usually served over meat and potatoes or mixed with beans for added flavor. This chapter includes a chowchow recipe handed down by longtime *Western Horseman* contributor Stella Hughes, a favorite with readers and a true woman of the West.

For more than 50 years, Stella connected with *Western Horseman* readers through her recipes and humorous articles about ranch life and camp catastrophes. Horseback daily with her husband, Mack, Stella still found time to cook for the crew, grow a garden, raise three children and contribute to her community–all without a telephone and electricity although a generator eventually provided that. She also started a business selling patterns to sew Western shirts. With no grocery store around the corner, Stella made the most of her homegrown produce, in season bringing it from the garden to the table and preserving any surplus for later use.

Her first article in *Western Horseman* appeared in the 1950s and recipes from her popular magazine column, "Bacon & Beans," later were compiled as a cookbook with the same title. An avid writer and camp cook, Stella's *Chuck Wagon Cookin'* was published in 1974 by the University of Arizona Press. A decade later, she released *Hashknife Cowboy*, a memoir of her husband, which won a Western Writers of America Spur Award for best nonfiction in 1984.

Stella died at age 92 in December 2008 on what would have been her and Mack's 70th wedding anniversary. Her legacy continues through the stories and recipes she has handed down to friends and family members. However, most soon realized that she rarely followed a recipe when cooking.

COCO/FIREFLY FOTOS, COURTESY PARELLI NATURAL HORSEMANSHIP

Asian Red Cabbage Salad

Deep purple and a little spicy if you wish!

Cabbage and Marinade
1 red cabbage
3 teaspoons sea salt
4 teaspoons vinegar (apple cider or wine vinegar)

Cut the cabbage in half and then thinly slice each half. Toss in a large bowl with sea salt and let stand for 10 to 30 minutes. Drizzle on the vinegar and toss cabbage again.

Dressing
2 tablespoons vinegar
3 tablespoons sesame oil
1 teaspoon honey
red pepper chili flakes—How hot do you want it?

Mix together the dressing ingredients and pour over the wilted cabbage.
Toss the cabbage and taste to check seasoning. Serve right away, or chill. Lasts a week.

Tip: If you don't want the salad Asian style, just use olive oil and vinegar for the dressing.

Linda Parelli
Pagosa Springs, Colorado

Aunt Jewel's Chowchow

JENNIFER DENISON

This recipe, passed along by industry icon Stella Hughes, had never been published until the January 2011 issue celebrating Western Horseman's 75th anniversary.

1 gallon ground green tomatoes
½ gallon ground cabbage
2 or 3 ground onions
½ gallon yellow apple cider vinegar
2 cups sugar
1 teaspoon cloves
1 teaspoon allspice
1 teaspoon cinnamon
1 teaspoon dry mustard
1 chopped bell pepper, optional
   Red or orange bell pepper adds color.
2 to 3 chopped hot peppers
1½ tablespoons salt
pepper to taste

Combine all ingredients and cook 30 minutes until the mixture is white in color. Can as usual. Serve over meats, pinto beans, baked sweet potatoes or hash browns.

Suzie Cox
Bloomfield, New Mexico

Wilted Lettuce Salad

This recipe, given to me by Susan Russell of the Russell Angus Ranch in Des Moines, New Mex., is really yummy, especially when served with her grass-fed beef.

4 slices diced bacon
¼ cup vinegar
2 bunches lettuce (Butter lettuce is
   really good!)

⅓ cup diced onion
2 teaspoons sugar
¼ teaspoon salt
⅛ teaspoon pepper

Fry bacon until crisp. Add vinegar and remove from heat. In a bowl, mix lettuce and onion; then sprinkle with everything else. Pour warm vinegar mix over all. Toss until lettuce is wilted and serve. Makes four servings.

Christine Hamilton
Fort Worth, Texas

Grape Salad

Colorful with a touch of rich sweetness and just the right amount of crunch!

4 cups green grapes
4 cups red grapes
1 8-ounce package cream cheese, softened
¼ cup sugar

¾ cup sour cream
1 tablespoon vanilla
brown sugar
crushed walnuts

Wash and stem grapes. Set aside.

Mix sour cream, cream cheese, white sugar and vanilla by hand until blended.

Stir grapes into mixture, and pour into a large serving bowl. Set aside.

For topping, combine brown sugar and crushed walnuts. Sprinkle over top of grapes to cover completely.

Chill salad for an hour before serving.

Kami Peterson
Elizabeth, Colorado

Summer-In-Your-Mouth Salad

One of my favorite side dishes. The fresh produce always tastes like summer in my mouth!

4 ears sweet corn, cooked with kernels cut off cob
1 pint grape or cherry tomatoes, cut in half
½ cup red onion, finely chopped
1 avocado, cut into ½-inch cubes
2 tablespoons olive oil
1 tablespoon freshly squeezed lime juice
zest from one lime
salt and freshly ground black pepper to taste
¼ cup chopped cilantro

Cook corn, cool, cut off kernels and place in mixing bowl. Add tomatoes, onion and chopped avocado.

In separate bowl, stir together olive oil, lime juice, zest, salt and pepper. Mix well. Then stir in chopped cilantro.

Pour the dressing over salad ingredients, stir gently and serve immediately.

Cynthia McFarland
Williston, Florida

Freelancer Cynthia McFarland, shown here with her "Ben," has written three Western Horseman *books—*Cow-Horse Confidence *with Martin Black,* Ride the Journey *with Chris Cox and* Horseman's Guide to Tack and Equipment.

STEVE FLOETHE

JENNIFER DENISON

Mediterranean Salad and Sangria

The balmy days of summer call for a light salad bursting with flavor and texture.
What better to pair with it than a fruity glass of fresh sangria?

Salad

3 tablespoons olive oil from ¾ cup total
  olive oil for both recipes
2 cloves garlic, minced
½ pound orzo
14 ounces chicken stock
1 lemon
1 head of lettuce or bag of mixed greens

2 cups grape or cherry tomatoes
½ cucumber, peeled and diced
½ zucchini, peeled and diced
1 cup pitted olives
½ cup feta cheese, crumbled
¼ cup dried cranberries
¼ cup pine nuts

In a medium saucepan, warm 3 tablespoons of olive oil over medium heat.
Add garlic and cook for 1 minute, until tender.

Add the orzo and toast until lightly browned, stirring often, for about 5 minutes.

Pour in chicken stock and the juice of one lemon, and bring to a boil. Reduce heat and simmer, covered,
until the orzo is tender and liquid is absorbed, stirring occasionally, about 20 minutes.

In a large salad bowl, gently toss all vegetables, cranberries, nuts, cheese and the orzo.

Dressing

¾ cup olive oil less 3 tablespoons
  used in preparing salad
¼ cup red wine vinegar
¾ tsp dried oregano, crumbled

¾ tsp dried basil, crumbled
salt and pepper to taste
1 lemon, juiced
1 lemon, zested

In a small bowl, mix together remaining olive oil, red wine vinegar,
herbs and seasonings for the salad dressing.

Drizzle dressing over the top of the salad.

Jennifer Denison
Sedalia, Colorado

Sangria

2 quarts Real Sangria
1 cup orange juice
1 cup pomegranate juice, optional
1 cup champagne
½ cup sweet red wine
3 limes
sliced fruit—oranges, pineapple, apples, mixed berries

Combine all ingredients in a pitcher and chill until ready to serve.

Joncee Blake
Weatherford, Texas

35

Mrs. Mac's Nine-Day Slaw

This coleslaw recipe from my mother-in-law, Martha McCraine,
can be made ahead of time and refrigerated for more than a week.

1 large head cabbage
1 bell pepper, finely chopped, or half
 green pepper and half red pepper
2 medium onions, finely chopped
2 cups plus 2 tablespoons sugar

¾ cup vegetable oil
¾ cup white vinegar
2 tablespoons salt
2 teaspoons celery seed

Shred cabbage in a food processor. Place in a large bowl and add chopped onion and bell pepper.
Blend in 2 cups sugar.

Blend remaining 2 tablespoons sugar with the rest of the ingredients
in a medium saucepan and bring to a full boil, stirring.

Pour mixture over the cabbage and stir. Let cool and refrigerate for up to nine days.

Kathy McCraine
Prescott, Arizona

From *Cow Country Cooking: Recipes and Tales From Northern Arizona's Historic Ranches*
by Kathy McCraine, Kathy McCraine Publisher, 2010.

Stella's Sweet and Sour Carrots

Here's Stella Hughes' unusual take on carrots as a side salad with Oriental flair.

Stella Hughes, shown here during a photo
shoot for Bacon & Beans, was inducted into
the National Cowgirl Hall of Fame in 1988.
WESTERN HORSEMAN ARCHIVES

1 pound carrots, diagonally sliced
1 medium green pepper, chopped
⅓ cup sugar
1 teaspoon corn starch
½ teaspoon salt
1 8-ounce can pineapple chunks
2 teaspoons vinegar
2 teaspoons soy sauce

Cook carrots, covered, in a small amount of salted boiling
water until tender. Add green pepper and cook 3 minutes,
then drain and set aside.

Combine sugar, cornstarch and salt in a medium-sized saucepan.
Drain pineapple, set aside and reserve juice.
Add enough water to reserved pineapple juice to make ⅓ cup
and stir into sugar mixture. Next, add the vinegar and soy sauce.
Cook over low heat until bubbly, stirring constantly.

Stir in vegetables and pineapple. Cook until thoroughly heated.
Yields 6 to 8 servings.

From *Bacon & Beans: A Collection of Tales and Recipes From the West*,
by Stella Hughes with Brenda Goodwin, *Western Horseman*, 1990.

Chili-Frito Corn Salad

This might not be considered a typical salad, but it's always is a huge hit with everyone!

4 cans corn, drained
1 green bell pepper, diced
1 red bell pepper, diced
½ red onion, chopped
8 ounces cheddar cheese
¾ cup mayonnaise
1 bag chili-flavored Fritos®

In a bowl, mix drained corn, diced green and red bell peppers, and onion. Add mayonnaise and cheese.

Right before serving, add the bag of chili-flavored Fritos to the salad ingredients. Mix all until well-coated. This will be a huge hit!

Kami Peterson
Elizabeth, Colorado

Hot Vinaigrette Salad

A delicious way to get your salad fix, complete with fresh produce and just-right seasonings!

Salad
approximately 8 cups green leaf lettuce, spinach or
  a combination of both
1 cucumber, chopped
1 cup tomatoes of choice—grape, cherry or chopped Roma
½ bell pepper, any color, coarsely chopped

Hot Dressing
2 slices bacon, cut into ½-inch pieces
2 tablespoons olive oil
1 medium onion, thinly sliced
2 tablespoons brown sugar
1 ½ cups sliced fresh mushrooms
salt and pepper to taste
2 tablespoons red wine vinegar
2 tablespoons balsamic vinegar

Fry bacon in olive oil until lightly crisped. Add onions and sauté until onions are semi-translucent. Add brown sugar and mushrooms, and continue to sauté over medium heat. Add vinegar and reduce heat to medium-low. Simmer until bubbly. Turn off heat and allow the dressing to rest for 3 to 5 minutes.

Slowly pour dressing over salad and toss until well-coated. Serve immediately.

Tip: You can also serve croutons or French bread with this salad.

Oda and Don Baskins
Tucumcari, New Mexico

Through the years, Don Baskins' clientele learned that the farrier and author of Well-Shod *appreciates fine food as much as he does nice horses.*

KATHY SWAN

37

Mexican Egg Salad

This healthy and wholesome egg-salad recipe is bursting with color and flavor.

1 dozen hard-boiled eggs, grated
1 ½ cups sharp cheddar cheese, grated
4 ribs celery, chopped
5 green onions, chopped
2 fresh jalapeños, chopped
½ green bell pepper, chopped
½ red bell pepper, chopped
1 cup mayonnaise
1 teaspoon garlic powder
1 teaspoon ground comino (cumin)
1 teaspoon chili powder
salt and pepper to taste
juice of one fresh lime

Combine first seven ingredients in a bowl and toss lightly.

Combine remaining ingredients in a separate bowl and mix well.

Pour the mayonnaise mixture over the egg mixture and blend well.
Cover and refrigerate overnight to blend flavors.

Serve on a bed of lettuce leaves and top with avocado slices.

Tip: You also can serve this egg salad on bread or crackers, or even stuff it in a tomato.

Robert Boyd
Trent, Texas

Avocado Tossed Salad

Not your average tossed salad, this chip-filled dish comes to life with a cowboy-pleasing, chili-powder, Tabasco-laced dressing.

Salad
1 head lettuce, rinsed and torn
   into bite-sized pieces
2 tomatoes, chopped
½ cup sliced ripe olives
2 green onions, chopped
½ cup shredded Cheddar cheese
1 cup crushed tortilla chips

Dressing
1 avocado, peeled and mashed
1 tablespoon lemon juice
½ cup sour cream
⅓ cup cooking oil
½ teaspoon seasoning salt, such as Lawry's
½ teaspoon sugar
½ teaspoon chili powder
¼ teaspoon salt
¼ teaspoon Tabasco®

Combine salad ingredients except for tortilla chips and set aside.

Combine dressing ingredients and mix until thoroughly blended.
Pour dressing to taste over salad ingredients and toss well. Add crushed chips just before serving.
Yield: 6 servings.

Tip: Men love this salad, and any leftover dressing is good as a dip, too.

Marianne McCartney
Throckmorton, Texas

From *Kitchen Keepsakes By Request*, by Bonnie Welch and Deanna White, Cookbook Publishers Inc., 1993.

Melitta's Broccoli Salad

What a flavorful combination—and a great "short-notice" salad to make when unexpected guests arrive!

Salad
4 cups broccoli florets
1 cup chopped celery
½ cup green onion, sliced
1 cup halved green grapes
1 cup halved red grapes
8 slices bacon, fried and crumbled
2/3 cup almonds, toasted

Combine salad ingredients in a large bowl and
mix well. Set aside and prepare dressing.

Dressing
1 cup mayonnaise
⅓ cup sugar
2 tablespoons vinegar

In a small bowl, mix mayonnaise,
sugar and vinegar thoroughly.

Pour dressing to taste
over salad ingredients and
toss well before serving.

Marsha Witte
Peyton, Colorado

Frosted 7-Up Fruit Salad

This refreshing, colorful salad, from a long line of ranch cowgirls in my family, has been a spring staple at many branding meals.

Salad

2 3-ounce packages lemon gelatin

2 cups boiling water

2 cups 7-Up

20-ounce can of crushed pineapple, drained well, set juice aside for topping

2 large bananas, sliced

2 small apples, chopped

1 cup nuts of your choice, finely chopped

1 cup miniature marshmallows

In a large bowl, dissolve gelatin in boiling water and add 7-Up.

Chill in refrigerator about 30 minutes, or until gelatin is partially set.

Stir in remaining ingredients, and chill until firm.

Topping

½ cup sugar

2 tablespoons flour

1 cup pineapple juice

¼ cup cheddar cheese, shredded

1 egg, beaten

2 tablespoons butter

1 cup whipped cream

Combine sugar and flour in a saucepan, and gradually stir in pineapple juice and egg. Cook on low heat, stirring constantly until thickened.

Stir in butter until melted, and then cool.

Fold in whipped cream, and then spread over set gelatin salad. Top with cheese.

Jennifer Denison
Sedalia, Colorado

JENNIFER DENISON

COCO/FIREFLY FOTOS, COURTESY PARELLI NATURAL HORSEMANSHIP

Roasted Red Peppers

Blackened, peeled, marinated! A classic Italian antipasto.

red bell peppers
salt
balsamic vinegar (Aged is best!)
olive oil
fresh basil
fresh oregano
garlic, finely chopped with sea salt, optional

Cut the bell peppers in half, lengthwise, and discard the seeds and stem.

Lay peppers on a baking sheet lined with aluminum foil and broil on high
until the skins are blackened and blistered—approximately 15 minutes.

Remove peppers from the oven and place in a plastic bag or covered pot to sweat and cool.

When cool, slip skins off the peppers. Working from the narrow end, push up from the bottom and,
using the flat of your thumb, slide the skin off in nice big strips.

Arrange peppers on a platter and sprinkle with salt. If using garlic, sprinkle that on now, too.

Drizzle on the vinegar and olive oil, in that order.

Garnish with basil and oregano and serve.

Tip: Although the peppers are ready to serve immediately, they also keep well in the fridge for up to 10
days. Just make sure the peppers are room temperature before serving.

Linda Parelli
Pagosa Springs, Colorado

43

Mandarin Orange Salad Greens

Mandarin oranges add style to the salad greens, and pecans and bacon add substance to each well-dressed bite. Plus, it's easy to prepare ahead of time.

Salad

salad greens
canned Mandarin oranges, well-drained
pecan pieces
cooked bacon, crumbled

Have enough salad greens and oranges
on hand to serve the number of people
you expect at the dinner table,
as well as enough chopped pecans and
cooked bacon to garnish each serving.

Dressing

⅓ cup lemon juice
⅔ cup cooking oil
½ cup sugar
2 teaspoons finely chopped onion
1 teaspoon salt
1 teaspoon paprika
2 dashes Worcestershire Sauce

Mix together dressing ingredients and
refrigerate for several hours before serving.

On a bed of salad greens, place slices of well-drained mandarin oranges,
topped with crumbled bacon and pecan pieces. Serve with dressing.

Marianne McCartney
Throckmorton, Texas

From *Cooking with St. Mary's*, St. Mary's Catholic Church, Graham, Texas, 1995.

Exotic Greens
with Strawberry Vinaigrette

This easy-to-make recipe is a flavor-filled treat, from the salad to the vinaigrette to the pine-nut and strawberry topping.

Salad

4 cups baby spinach
4 cups butter lettuce
2 cups cherry tomatoes

Mix salad greens and tomatoes well in large bowl
and set aside.

Toppings

¼ cup toasted pine nuts
6 whole strawberries, fanned
2 ounces goat cheese

Vinaigrette

8 ounces frozen strawberries
¼ cup sugar
1 teaspoon balsamic vinegar
1 teaspoon rice wine vinegar
⅓ cup olive oil
⅓ cup soybean oil
¼ teaspoon salt
¼ teaspoon white pepper

Process strawberries in blender until pureed.
Then add sugar, vinegars, oils and seasonings,
and process until blended.

Pour vinaigrette over salad and toss together. Garnish salad with toppings before serving.

Dalene Cameron
Bluff Dale, Texas

JENNIFER DENISON

Idaho's Bean & Pasta Salad

This easy-to-make salad recipe includes an equally easy-to-make dressing with low-fat ingredients.

Salad

1½ cups cooked or canned red beans

2 cups small-shell macaroni, cooked and drained

2 cups frozen peas and carrots, thawed and drained

1½ cups sliced celery

Combine macaroni, beans, peas, carrots and celery and mix well. Set aside.

Dressing

¼ cup low-fat Italian dressing

¼ cup low-fat mayonnaise

2 tablespoons chopped parsley

½ teaspoon salt

⅛ teaspoon pepper

Mix Italian dressing, mayonnaise, parsley, salt and pepper in separate bowl.

Toss dressing with the macaroni mixture. Mix well. Serves eight.

Dirk Kempthorne
Sun Valley, Idaho

From *Boots 'n' Beans* by Boots Reynolds, courtesy of the Reynolds family and Keokee Co. Publishing, 2008.

Patriotic Salad

*This fruity, three-layer dessert salad can add a little red, white and blue
to your Fourth of July barbecue.*

Layer One

1 3-ounce package of strawberry gelatin

Prepare gelatin per package instructions and pour
into a 9-by-13-inch cake pan and chill until set.

Layer Two

1 envelope unflavored gelatin
½ cup cold water
1 cup half-and-half
1 cup sugar
1 teaspoon vanilla
2 cups sour cream

Combine gelatin and ½ cup cold water. Whip in
other ingredients until smooth.
Pour mixture over the already set strawberry
gelatin, and chill until set.

Layer Three

1 3-ounce package raspberry gelatin
1 cup blueberries
1 cup juice from blueberries

Prepare gelatin per package instructions,
except add up to 1 cup blueberry juice in
place of cold water. Gently stir in blueberries.
Pour mixture over the first two layers,
and chill until set.

When the gelatin has molded, cut into squares
and serve on lettuce leaves.

Tip: In December, I change my mother's red,
white, and blue salad recipe above and
make it with red and green layers for
the Christmas season.

Betty Cornforth
Caldwell, Idaho

JENNIFER DENISON

JENNIFER DENISON

Poppy Seed-Almond Chicken Salad

Enjoy this salad's flavor, color and texture as a light lunch or appetizer.

Salad

3 cups boiled chicken, chopped
½ cup chopped celery
½ cup chopped red onion
½ cup seedless red grapes, halved lengthwise
1 cup fresh pineapple, cubed
2 ounces sliced, toasted almonds

Toss together the salad ingredients, adding salt and pepper to taste. Set aside.

Dressing

½ cup mayonnaise
½ cup poppy-seed dressing
salt and pepper

In a separate bowl, combine mayonnaise and poppy-seed dressing, mixing well.

Pour the dressing mixture over the chicken mixture and stir well.
Cover and refrigerate overnight to combine flavors.

Serve over a bed of lettuce leaves with crackers, and top with slivered almonds.

Robert Boyd
Trent, Texas

47

JENNIFER DENISON

Western-Mexi Salad

*After a busy day on the ranch and with many hungry mouths to feed,
you can quickly toss together this salad and dressing.*

Salad

1-pound bag iceberg lettuce
10 ounces romaine lettuce
1½ cups cheddar cheese
1 4-ounce can sliced olives
1 15-ounce can kidney beans, rinsed and drained
½ cup onion
1 red bell pepper, chopped
1 green bell pepper, chopped
1 tomato, chopped
1 avocado, sliced
8 ounces Nacho Cheese Doritos®, crumbled

Dressing

¾ cup mayonnaise
¾ cup sour cream
¼ cup ranch dressing
½ package taco seasoning
½ cup salsa

Combine all salad ingredients in a bowl and toss well.

In a separate bowl, mix together all dressing ingredients.

Pour dressing over the salad to taste. Toss dressing into salad and serve.

Tip: For a heartier salad, add cooked ground beef or strips of grilled chicken or steak.

Jeannie Amen
Nampa, Idaho

Jerry Baird, who has served food from his chuck wagon for several decades, helped establish the American Chuck Wagon Association.

ROSS HECOX

On a Roll

The chuck wagon was invented in Texas in 1866, when legendary cattleman Charles Goodnight nailed a stout chuck box onto the back of an Army-surplus wagon. From that humble beginning, the rolling commissary went on to become a widely recognized symbol of cattle roundups and the cowboy lifestyle. Consequently, Jerry Baird of Snyder, Texas, felt it only appropriate that his home state recognize the historic horse-drawn kitchen.

To that end, Baird helped found the American Chuck Wagon Association, and in 2006 he was instrumental in getting his favorite four-wheeler named the Official Vehicle of Texas.

"David Holt and I, and some of the chuck-wagon association people, got together and started an effort to make the chuck wagon the Official Vehicle of Texas," Baird says. "To get something like this done, I had to go to Austin [the state capital] for hearings. Owen Noble and I testified before the Senate House committee. Then it had to be voted on by the Senate, then the governor had to sign it. It's just like trying to pass a law."

Baird has cooked out of a chuck wagon for more than 30 years. Working from his century-old wagon, he prepares meals for ranch gatherings, caters special events and has won several chuck-wagon cook-off competitions. Recently, he began marketing his own line of special seasonings.

The American Chuck Wagon Association was established to preserve the range cook's heritage. The organization is now made up of more than 150 wagons across the country, from Texas to Oregon.

"We had no idea it would grow like it did," Baird says. "Through the years, it's continued to expand. All of a sudden, people got interested. They started finding those old wagons, rebuilding them and fixing them up. [The chuck wagon] was a part of history in the ranching industry that was just about to fade away."

Learn more about the American Chuck Wagon Association, upcoming competitive events, cook-off results, membership and youth activities by visiting americanchuckwagon.org.

—Ross Hecox

MAIN DISHES 3

Cowboy culture, from its folk songs to its chuck-wagon fare, evolved from other cultures around the world. The cowboys who rode up the trail were former Civil War soldiers, freed slaves, Hispanics and even Irish immigrants. These tough men signed up to drive cattle through rough terrain and hostile Indian Territory for only about $1 per day.

Main dishes in cowboy cuisine of past and present have been developed from recipes shared from around the world. A Hispanic cook probably used more chili peppers in his dishes, while African-American cooks brought sweet potatoes, beans, rice and other staples prevalent in the South. Irish stew was a favorite on the wagon, but rather than use the lamb, as in the traditional recipe, the cowboys substituted wild game or beef. Many of the main courses served up in this chapter have Hispanic origins, including the tamale recipe from Darrell Dodds, former *Western Horseman* publisher.

Tamales can be used as a heavy appetizer or main course. Developed by the Aztecs, tamales were prepared for religious ceremonies and still are commonly given as gifts during the holidays in the Southwest. Many ways to prepare tamales and recipes have been handed down for generations, but the most common version in cowboy cuisine is the traditional cornhusk-wrapped tamale. Most tamale recipes, including Darrell's, are versatile, so you can experiment with heat from peppers to find what suits your taste.

"I'm a firm believer that good tamales should produce a little sweat on your upper lip and forehead to be fully appreciated," says Darrell, who lives in Texas.

Whatever main course you choose to cook, it's important to remember that this dish is the heart of the meal and the foundation around which all sides are selected. A delectable main dish makes a meal memorable, while poorly prepared fare can cause a meal to flop.

Any type of meat can be braised, smoked, fried or grilled to perfection. However, don't forget the convenience of casseroles you can freeze ahead of time and pop in the oven, or soups, green or red chilies, and other hearty slow-cooker meals that can simmer all day and be ready to serve when everyone gets home or gets hungry.

JENNIFER DENISON

Chicken Mexicalli

*This flavorful, filling and colorful Southwestern-inspired dish
has graced the Deming family table for three generations.*

3-pound whole chicken
1 green pepper, chopped
1 onion, chopped
1 10 ¾-ounce can cream of mushroom soup
1 10 ¾-ounce can cream of chicken soup
1 10-ounce can Ro*Tel® tomatoes
8 ounces tortilla chips
8 ounces shredded cheese

Preheat oven to 350 degrees.

Place chicken in a stockpot filled with water and boil until meat is cooked throughout.
Debone and shred chicken, and dip out one cup of chicken broth and set aside.

Spread tortilla chips evenly in the bottom of a 9-by-13-inch casserole dish,
and top with an even layer of chicken.

In a mixing bowl, combine green pepper, onion, soups, tomatoes and chicken broth.
Pour mixture over chicken and tortilla chips.

Top casserole with cheese, and bake at 350 degrees for 45 minutes or until done.

Tip: As with any recipe, you need the major ingredients, but you have the option
of seasoning it to your taste. With this recipe, you can substitute ground or
shredded beef for the chicken, and can spice it up with green chilies and/or jalapeños.

Jacquelyn Deming
Fredericksburg, Texas

Green Chili

This recipe traveled from New Mexico to Colorado, where it has become a favorite among horsemen along Colorado's Front Range.

2 cups cold water
4 tablespoons flour
1 pound meat—pork chops, chicken, etc.
1 medium onion, diced
4 medium potatoes, diced

1 15 ½-ounce can peeled tomatoes
garlic salt, salt and pepper
8 Anaheim chilies roasted, peeled
   and chopped
1 15 ½-ounce cans pinto beans

In a bowl, mix the flour and cold water. Stir well until smooth and then set aside.

Cook the meat, onion and potatoes.

Add the flour and water mixture, stirring well. Then add tomatoes and season to taste with salt, pepper and garlic salt.

Cook for 1 to 2 hours over low heat, stirring frequently.

About 15 minutes before serving, add roasted chilies and pinto beans.

Don Baskins
Tucumcari, New Mexico

Chicken and Green Chilies Casserole

Hearty and filling, this recipe can be prepared ahead and frozen for use later when your day is jam-packed.

4 tablespoons butter
1 onion, chopped
3 tablespoons flour
2 cups milk
1 cup chicken broth
1 4-ounce can green chilies,
   seeded and chopped

1 ½ teaspoons salt
½ can, 10-ounce Ro*Tel® tomatoes
   with green chilies
2 pounds cooked chicken, deboned
   and cut into pieces
12 tortillas, torn into small pieces
1 pound sharp cheddar cheese, grated

Preheat oven to 375 degrees.

In a heavy pan or skillet, melt butter. Then add onion and sauté 1 minute. Add flour and cook until bubbly, stirring often. Pour in milk and broth. Cook and stir frequently until casserole sauce has thickened. Mix green chilies and salt with the sauce and add tomatoes.

Place a layer of chicken in the bottom of a buttered, shallow 3-quart casserole dish. Add layers of tortillas, cheese and sauce. Then repeat layers, reserving enough cheese to sprinkle on top as final layer.
Bake at 375 degrees until casserole is bubbling.

Tip: Prepare the casserole whenever it's convenient and refrigerate or even freeze it before baking.

Tonya Ward
Weatherford, Texas

A Boots Hill recipe from *Tasteful Traditions*, Women for Abilene Christian University, 1983, now out of print.

Bierocks

These meat-filled pastries are easy to prepare. Cooked at home and frozen, they are easily reheated over campfire coals.

1 pound ground beef
1 pound bulk sausage
1 large onion, chopped
1 large jar sauerkraut, drained well
2 cups shredded cheddar cheese
1 cup prepared mustard
salt and pepper to taste
2 premade piecrusts, canned biscuits, crescent rolls or bread dough
1 egg, beaten

Preheat oven to 425 degrees.

Brown meat and onions. Add other ingredients and mix thoroughly.

Roll out dough on a floured surface and cut out circles in whatever sizes you want, using glasses, bowls or a biscuit cutter. Place a spoonful of the meat mixture on half the dough circle and fold remaining dough over. Seal the edges by pressing them down with your fingers or a fork.

Brush dough with egg and bake on a greased cookie sheet at 425 degrees until golden brown.

Tip: The bierocks can be made ahead of time and frozen. If you wrap them in aluminum foil, you can throw the package onto hot campfire coals to heat.

Becky Prunty Lisle
Charleston, Nevada

Sheryl's Favorite Brisket

Braise a brisket that is flavorful and fall-apart tender.

4 large onions, chopped
2 large sweet peppers, chopped
1 3- to 5-pound brisket, trimmed
1 can beer
¾ cup chili sauce
3 tablespoons brown sugar
2 to 4 garlic cloves, minced
mustard, a healthy squirt to taste
1 hot pickled chili pepper, minced with juice
2 tablespoons chili powder, or to taste
1 teaspoon salt
½ teaspoon pepper

Place onions and peppers on the bottom of a pan or Dutch oven and top with meat.

In a bowl, combine beer, chili sauce, brown sugar, garlic, mustard, chili pepper and juice, chili powder, salt and pepper. Pour mixture over meat.

Cook on low heat for 5 to 6 hours.

Rex and Sheryl Wailes
Bennett, Colorado

JENNIFER DENISON

Turkey Pot Pie

Tired of turkey? Sick of sandwiches?
Clean up Thanksgiving leftovers with
this quick and hearty pot-pie recipe.

5 potatoes, peeled and cubed
½ onion, chopped
15 ounces frozen peas
1 ¼ pounds shredded turkey
8 to 10 cut-out biscuits, purchased
    or homemade

Preheat oven to 350 degrees.

Place potatoes and onion in a pot of boiling
water, and cook until tender. Add turkey,
peas, salt, and pepper to taste.

While the meat and vegetables heat, create
a thickening of two to three tablespoons
of flour and equal parts of cold water.
Whisk mixture well, removing lumps. Add
thickening to pot-pie mixture and stir well.

Place mixture in a casserole dish or Dutch
oven, then top with biscuits. Brush melted
butter over biscuits.

Bake at 350 degrees until biscuits
are golden brown.

Jennifer Denison
Sedalia, Colorado

Campfire Spaghetti and Meatballs

Decades ago, a dear friend shared this recipe—her husband's favorite, especially when prepared by the "chuck-wagon cook" on a campfire stove during their hunting trips back in the 1940s.

Meatballs

¾ cup dried bread crumbs
¾ cup milk
1 ½ pounds ground round
½ pound pork shoulder, ground
½ teaspoon black pepper
1 ½ teaspoons salt
¼ teaspoon nutmeg

Soak dried bread crumbs and milk together.

Mix well with remaining ingredients and form into balls.

Brown meatballs in a skillet. Then remove and set aside.

Sauce

1 tablespoon butter
2 onions, finely chopped
½ green pepper, finely chopped
1 teaspoon chopped parsley
1 pimento, canned or fresh, finely chopped
1 large can cream of mushroom soup
2 cups tomato puree
1 small can tomato soup
1 small can tomato sauce
¼ cup ketchup
½ teaspoon allspice
½ teaspoon oregano
1 teaspoon Beau Monde
1 tablespoon Worcestershire sauce
½ teaspoon garlic powder
½ teaspoon black pepper
1 tablespoon sugar

Professional horsewoman Deanna Lally co-authored The Art of Hackamore Training *with Al Dunning and Benny Guitron, and since has written another* Western Horseman *book about working cow horses with Al.*

JOHN SPARKES

Using a large kettle, sauté butter, onions, pepper and parsley together until tender.

Add remaining sauce ingredients and simmer on low heat for 30 minutes.

Add meatballs to sauce and simmer on low for 1 hour.

Serve over spaghetti noodles and sprinkle with Parmesan cheese. Enjoy!

Deanna Lally
Snohomish, Washington

59

Tex-Mex Cornbread Pie

*Hamburger night takes on a new meaning with this simple recipe
made from ingredients you probably have on hand.*

1 pound ground beef
½ cup chopped onion
½ chopped bell pepper, optional
salt and pepper to taste
½ teaspoon cumin
1 can of whole kernel corn, drained

1 can Ranch-Style Beans, undrained, or any saucy
  bean, such as Bush's Smokehouse Tradition Beans
cornbread batter, homemade or packaged mix
½ cup of chopped jalapeños
2 cups grated cheddar cheese

Preheat oven to 425 degrees.
Brown ground beef with onions, bell pepper, salt, pepper and cumin, then drain.

In a 9-by-13 cake pan, mix browned ground beef and onion, drained corn and beans.
Top this mixture with the cheese.

In a separate bowl, mix cornbread and add jalapeños to the cornbread mix. Drizzle cornbread mix over the
meat mixture in the cake pan. The cornbread might not cover all of the pan contents. You can gently spread
the cornbread mixture with a spoon, and as the cornbread cooks, it will spread and rise.

Bake for 15 to 20 minutes or until cornbread is golden brown.

Teresa and Bobby Burleson
Weatherford, Texas

Beef Tenderloin

If you love your grill, you'll love this simple, tasty tenderloin recipe!

beef tenderloin
1 bottle Italian dressing
1 package brown gravy mix

Preheat outdoor grill to a high temperature, about 475 degrees.

Marinate the tenderloin in Italian dressing for at least 2 hours; 4 hours is best.

Drain marinade from meat. Rub or pat about half the dry gravy mix into the meat. Use your own judgment
about the amount, as the mix is what makes the crust on the tenderloin.

Place the tenderloin on the grill for no more than 20 minutes, being sure to turn the meat to seal the juices
inside. Then insert a meat thermometer, which should read about 130 degrees for medium-rare beef.

Take the tenderloin off the grill and wrap the meat in aluminum foil, which allows the meat to continue
cooking. Then set tenderloin aside for about 10 minutes of "hang time" before serving.

Carol Laramore Gipson
Eaton, Colorado

Sarsaparilla Soda Burgers

Fire up the grill and go beyond basic burgers.

Sauce

½ teaspoon garlic powder or
  two cloves minced garlic

1 small onion, minced

½ small bell pepper, minced

2 tablespoons olive oil

1 cup ketchup

½ cup sarsaparilla or Dr Pepper

1 tablespoon Worcestershire sauce

1 teaspoon cayenne

1 teaspoon dry mustard

1 teaspoon cumin

½ teaspoon salt

½ teaspoon pepper

To make the sauce, sauté onions, garlic and bell pepper in olive oil in a saucepan. When onions and bell peppers are tender, add remaining ingredients. Bring mixture to a boil and cook for 5 minutes, stirring frequently.

Burgers

1 pound ground beef or game

½ cup crushed pretzels

1 egg, beaten

In a mixing bowl, combine meat, pretzel crumbs and egg, and mix with your hands. Add ¼ cup of sauce to the meat mixture and mix well. Divide meat into four equal portions and form patties.

Grill patties on each side for 5 minutes or until meat is cooked to preference. Brush each side of each patty with remaining sauce while grilling.

Place the burgers on buns, garnish and serve.

Jennifer Denison
Sedalia, Colorado

JENNIFER DENISON

61

Tamales

No matter how hot—or not—you prefer your tamales,
this time-tested recipe truly is a season-to-taste main dish!

My recipe for making tamales is pretty generic. There are many different versions, of course;
I think every region in Mexico has a variation of ingredients and preparation methods.
One of the nice things about making tamales is that you can experiment until you find a recipe that fits your taste and tolerance of heat. I usually make two slightly different recipes at Christmas, one to give away to friends and another, slightly hotter version for myself. I'm a firm believer that good tamales should produce a little sweat on your upper lip and forehead to be fully appreciated. The recipe provided here produces a tasty, but not too hot, tamale perfect for most people.

Red Chili Sauce

16 dried California chilies
water
3 tablespoons lard or vegetable oil
2 garlic cloves
2 tablespoons all-purpose flour
2 teaspoons vinegar
2 teaspoons salt
1 teaspoon crushed dried leaf oregano
1 teaspoon cumin
½ teaspoon garlic powder

Prepare Red Chili Sauce a day in advance while the pork for the tamale filling cooks.

Combine all chili sauce ingredients and set aside until pork is cooked and has been pulled.

Tip: For a hotter variety of chili sauce, substitute New Mexico chilies for California chilies.

Pork Tamale Filling

2 pounds pork butt
5 cups water
1 medium onion
2 garlic cloves
3 bay leaves
salt to taste
12 peppercorns
2 cups red chili sauce

Although you can substitute beef or chicken, pork is more traditional and pairs well with the red chili sauce. Regardless of the meat you choose, prepare the filling a day in advance to make these mildly seasoned tamales.

A day in advance, trim fat from meat. Place meat in a Crockpot or pressure cooker and add water, onion, garlic, bay leaf, salt to taste and peppercorns. Cook until meat is tender enough to pull apart easily with two forks.

Drain meat, reserving broth for tamale dough.

With two forks, shred meat; then mix meat with prepared chili sauce. Refrigerate meat mixture and reserved broth overnight.

Tamale Dough

4 cups instant masa

2 teaspoons baking powder

1 teaspoon salt

3 cups lukewarm reserved pork broth or water

1½ cup lard or vegetable shortening

Combine instant masa, baking powder and salt in a large bowl. Work broth or water into the masa with your fingers, making a soft moist dough.

In a small bowl, beat lard or shortening until fluffy. Add to masa and beat until dough has a spongy texture. This recipe makes enough dough for about 24 medium-sized tamales.

Tip: If you live in an area with a sizable Hispanic population, you can save yourself a lot of time by buying fresh tamale dough at your local grocery store. If you are not so lucky, you can make your own by following the recipe.

Assembly

cornhusks or foil wrapping for 24 tamales

If using cornhusks, soak in hot water for 1 hour.

To assemble tamales, hold each cornhusk with the point toward you. Place a rounded tablespoon of dough at large end of husk and spread with small spatula. Place one large tablespoon of pork filling on the dough, then fold sides of husk over the tamale. Fold pointed end of cornhusk under the seam on outside.

Stand tamales on folded ends on a rack over water in a large pot. Cover with additional husks and bring water to a boil, then reduce heat. Cover and steam for 1 hour or until dough pulls easily from husk.

Darrel Dodds
Krum, Texas

Lifelong photographer and equine journalist Darrell Dodds, shown here on "Holly," retired as Western Horseman *publisher to enjoy his photography and horses full-time.*

Mama Mia Meatloaf

This recipe has all the heartiness and goodness of your mother's traditional meatloaf,
but with a spicy kick.

1 pound spicy Italian sausage
1 pound ground beef
1 onion, finely chopped
1 green pepper, finely chopped
2 cloves garlic, chopped
½ cup chopped green chilies
1 egg, beaten

1 tablespoon Worcestershire sauce
1 teaspoon cayenne pepper
salt and pepper to taste
½ cup Italian breadcrumbs
1 cup corn tortillas, chopped
3 tablespoons steak sauce

Preheat oven to 400 degrees.

In a large bowl, mix sausage and ground beef. Add remaining ingredients,
but set aside 2 tablespoons of steak sauce.

Knead the mixture until all ingredients are blended. Shape mixture into a loaf
and place in a baking pan coated with cooking spray. Drizzle remaining steak sauce over meatloaf.

Bake 1½ to 2 hours, until cooked thoroughly.

Tip: Use pan drippings as a gravy base to top the meatloaf. With this recipe, you can substitute
ground turkey for the beef and/or sausage, and you can add hot sauce,
jalapeños or other fiery fixings to suit your taste.

Jennifer Denison
Sedalia, Colorado

JENNIFER DENISON

Mexican Vermicelli

This pasta dish originated in a New Mexico ranch cookhouse in the 1960s.
Serve with a tossed salad and warm bread for a tasty, filling meal.

2 tablespoons shortening
½ pound vermicelli
1 to 1 ½ pounds ground beef
1 teaspoon salt
1 teaspoon pepper
1 teaspoon chili powder
dash of garlic powder

2 cups onions, diced
2 cups celery, chopped
½ cup green pepper, chopped
1-pound can of stewed or diced tomatoes
1 ½ cups whole-kernel corn
1 cup water
8 slices of any type of cheese

Brown vermicelli in shortening, breaking the pasta into small pieces. Stir in meat and brown, draining excess fat. Add remaining ingredients and blend.

Cook on stovetop over low heat for 25 minutes.
Prior to serving, place cheese slices on top and allow them to melt.

Judy Howell
Morill, Nebraska

JENNIFER DENISON

Drunken Roast Beef

The Circle F chuck wagon in Petersburg, Texas, originally came up with this recipe, which was modified for the Heavirland wagon.

cooking oil
1 beef roast
1 12-ounce can beer
1 package dry Italian dressing mix
potatoes and vegetables of choice
1 shot liquid smoke
1 large onion, chopped in eighths

Add thin coating of oil to Dutch oven, and brown roast on all sides.

Slowly add the beer and dressing mix. Cook for 2 ½ hours, changing coals as needed to maintain about 300 degrees. Add more beer as needed, and drink the rest.

Add the liquid smoke and vegetables, and cook for about 45 minutes or until tender.

Tip: This is another recipe that easily makes the transition from the chuck-wagon campfire to your kitchen.

Robert Heavirland
North Branch, Minnesota

As adapted from the Circle F recipe in *Second Helpings*, American Chuck Wagon Association, 2008.

Cowboy Coffee Tri-Tip

A little java and a splash of red wine bring out the rich flavors of beef's natural juices.

3- to 4-pound tri-tip or
  other type of beef roast
2 tablespoons olive oil
1 medium yellow onion, sliced in quarters
1 cup sliced mushrooms
4 garlic cloves, sliced in half
2 bay leaves

2 sprigs thyme
1 tablespoon tomato paste
2 cups prepared cowboy coffee
2 cups water
1 tablespoon butter
½ cup red wine

JENNIFER DENISON

Preheat oven to 400 degrees.

Heat oil in a heavy-duty roasting pan
or Dutch oven. Sear roast on all sides.
Add all ingredients to pan
except butter and wine.

Cover and roast for 1½ to 2 hours, or until
the meat is cooked to your liking.
Remove meat from pan and slice. Discard
bay leaves and thyme sprigs.

Combine butter, wine and pan juices, and
heat to a boil. Serve the au jus on the side or
over the meat.

Tip: This recipe also can be prepared
in a slow-cooker.

Jennifer Denison
Sedalia, Colorado

Marilyn's Porcupine Balls

My husband, Tim, really likes these — one of his favorites!

1 pound lean ground beef
½ cup uncooked white rice
1 can chopped green chilies

1 8-ounce can tomato sauce
1 cup water

Preheat oven to 350 degrees.

In a large bowl, combine the ground beef, rice and can of green chilies. Mix well.
Shape meat mixture into 1½-inch balls.

In a large skillet over medium heat, brown the meatballs; then drain fat.

In a covered baking dish, combine the tomato sauce and 1 cup of water.
Then place the browned meatballs in the tomato sauce, turning to coat well.

Cover and bake in a preheated oven for 60 minutes.

Suzie Cox
Bloomfield, New Mexico

Cowboy Crock-Pot Beef, Beans and Bacon with Confetti Relish

Warm up your working crew with this quick and easy chuck-wagon-inspired meal.

Cowboy Crock-Pot Beef, Beans and Bacon

1 pound ground beef
¾ to 1 pound bacon
1 cup onions, chopped
2 15-ounce cans pork and beans with liquid
2 16-ounce cans Ranch or pinto beans, drained
1 cup ketchup
¼ cup brown sugar
1 tablespoon liquid smoke
3 tablespoons white vinegar

Slice bacon into 1-inch pieces. In a skillet, brown bacon, ground beef and onions, and drain. Place meat and onions in a slow-cooker and add beans.

In a small bowl, combine ketchup, brown sugar, liquid smoke and vinegar. Add to the slow-cooker. Stir well and cook on low for 4 to 9 hours.

Tip: This traditional chuck-wagon-style dish also can be cooked in a Dutch oven over a campfire. Great sides to this hearty main dish include cornbread, coleslaw, potato salad, sliced tomatoes and Confetti Relish.

Confetti Relish

1 medium onion, coarsely chopped
10 ounces frozen, mixed vegetables, thawed
½ cup cider vinegar
⅓ cup water
3 tablespoons sugar
½ teaspoon mustard seed
½ teaspoon salt
⅛ teaspoon hot-pepper sauce

In a 2-cup jar or small bowl, combine onion and vegetables; then set aside.

In a small saucepan, mix remaining ingredients and bring to a boil.
Reduce heat and simmer 5 minutes.

Pour mixture over vegetables. Cover and refrigerate for at least 2 hours.

Fran Devereux Smith
Fort Worth, Texas

JENNIFER DENISON

Hearty Beef and Noodles

Country living often means preparing meals with ingredients on hand. This recipe, handed down from my mother, is simple to prepare and satisfying on a cold winter day.

3 cups flour
1 teaspoon salt
4 eggs
⅓ cup water
1 pound shredded chuck roast or beef stew meat, cooked
½ cup chopped onion
1 14-ounce can beef broth
1 12-ounce jar brown gravy
pepper to taste

Combine flour and salt in large bowl, and set aside.

In another bowl, beat eggs and water. Pour egg mixture into dry ingredients and stir well, forming a stiff dough.

Place dough on well-floured surface and roll out to ⅛-inch thickness. Let dry, then cut dough into strips with a pizza cutter.

In a stockpot, combine beef, onion, broth and gravy, and bring to a boil. Add noodles and boil 30 to 45 minutes until tender. Season with pepper and serve.

Tip: We like to serve beef and noodles with mashed potatoes and green beans.

Jennifer Denison
Sedalia, Colorado

JENNIFER DENISON

Chili Verde

Cultural and culinary traditions meld with flavor in this recipe. Make it as a main meal or as a topping for other Mexican dishes.

¼ cup vegetable oil
2 medium onions, cut into strips
2 garlic bulbs, minced
8-pound pork roast, cubed
2 pounds green chilies, cut into strips
3 bunches of green onions, cut into strips
2 bunches of cilantro, chopped

2 limes
2 tablespoons coarse salt
4 tablespoons cumin
2 tablespoons lemon pepper
¼ cup cornstarch
¼ cup milk

Add oil to a 14-inch deep Dutch oven and preheat with 14 coals on top and on the bottom when cooking on the campfire.

Sauté onions and garlic in the Dutch oven until caramelized, about 7 minutes. Check and stir once or twice so they don't burn.

Add the cubed pork and brown, stirring well. Cook covered for about 30 minutes, checking and stirring regularly to be sure the broth is cooking at a high simmer. If broth is not forming, add 2 cups of warm water. Have extra coals started to maintain the heat, and don't be afraid to add coals as needed to keep things hot.

Stir green chilies and cilantro into the meat, allowing the broth to simmer 1 hour and stirring regularly. Then add the spices and lime juice, and simmer 30 minutes.

In a bowl, whisk milk into the cornstarch until there are no lumps. Stir quickly into the middle of the chili to keep lumps from forming, and then blend completely. The mixture will thicken as it simmers. If it becomes too thick, add milk. Add cornstarch to thicken.

Simmer until meat is completely tender before serving.

Tip: This recipe easily can be adapted for cooking at home in the kitchen. You also can add diced tomatoes and beef to the chili.

Barbara Kennedy
Desert Hills, Arizona

JENNIFER DENISON

Five Dutch-Oven Cooking Tips

JOHN BRASSEAUX

For most people, the only place to experience chuck-wagon cuisine and culture is at a catered party or chuck-wagon cooking contest, such as the one held during the Western Heritage Classic in Abilene, Texas. Texan Tom Perini has promoted the heritage of this traditional culinary art. The cowboy cook travels with his 1850s chuck wagon to cowboy festivals, rodeo events and other functions throughout the West. His Dutch-oven demonstrations often inspire spectators to go home and try some of his tips.

Perini admits that Dutch-oven cooking is difficult, but says you shouldn't be daunted by it.

"Just remember that one of the most important things is your fire," he says. Once you get a feel for cooking over coals, it gets easier. "And," he adds, "even the best cooks have burned their biscuits."

Here, Perini offers five tips to remember when cooking your favorite Dutch-oven recipe.

1. Plan your pit. Dig your fire pit in an area away from potential water runoff. If it were to rain, you don't want the water to extinguish your only heat source. You also can build up dirt around the fire pit to deflect runoff.

2. Gather hardwood. In the days of cattle drives, cowboys picked up firewood along the trail and placed the wood in a rawhide sack, called a coosie, which hung under the wagon bed. In treeless areas, cow chips fueled the campfire. Today, chuck-wagon cooks prefer the high heat and long-burning coals produced by hardwoods, such as mesquite.

3. Watch the weather. If the ground is wet, it's difficult to start a fire. If it's windy, gusts could fan your coals, creating hotspots. One way to overcome the elements is to put heated coals in the bottom of a metal washtub, a staple on any chuck wagon, and set your Dutch oven on top of the coals. The washtub serves as a windshield.

4. Feed the fire. When you shovel out coals, be sure to add more wood to maintain your heat source until you're finished cooking. During the chuck wagon's heyday, cowboys roped and dragged a big log to the campfire each night. As the "night log" burned, cowboys inched it farther into the fire. The next morning, the coals were ready for the cookie to start the coffee and that day's meal.

5. Rotate your pot and lid. The biggest mistake people make when cooking over campfires is putting too many coals beneath Dutch ovens, which is akin to turning up an oven burner. To avoid burning food, place coals beneath the Dutch oven and on the lid. Every 10 minutes, turn the Dutch oven and lid 90 degrees to prevent a hotspot from ruining your recipe. Also, frequently remove the lid and make sure you're not overcooking your food.

Tom Perini worked on West Texas ranches, cowboying and cooking, before using his culinary skills to open Perini Ranch Steakhouse in Buffalo Gap.

ROSS HECOX

Tom Perini is the author of *Texas Cowboy Cooking* and the owner of Perini Ranch Steakhouse and Guest Quarters in Buffalo Gap, Texas.

SIDE DISHES 4

Some foods just naturally go together, such as hamburgers and French fries, brisket and coleslaw, and pork chops and applesauce. In traditional chuck-wagon cooking, meat main courses partner well with potatoes and beans. At chuck-wagon cook-offs held by the American Chuck Wagon Association and other organizations, the wagon teams compete in standard food categories—meat, bread, beans, potatoes and desserts—as well as having their wagons judged for authenticity. The judges get samples of the same foods, but cooked in myriad ways, yet the dishes still complement each other as a full meal.

Mating a main course with appropriate side dishes can add variety to a meal, can balance it nutritionally and can make it more appetizing. When selecting sides, it's important to choose one that complements your main dish, but does not compete with or overpower it. Sides should spruce up the flavor and appearance of meats and other main courses, making your entire meal a big hit with your crew.

A good side dish also can be served alone as a main course. For example, the recipe for Green Beans and New Potatoes is a favorite meal for *Western Horseman*'s Senior Editor Jennifer Denison, especially when green beans and potatoes are fresh from the garden. Not only do the flavors of the vegetables meld well, they also are enhanced with bits of bacon; the fare is a complete meal with a protein, vegetables and a starch.

The other beautiful thing about side dishes is that a cook can be creative and experiment with unconventional ingredients. Most cowboys probably haven't tried couscous, but in other parts of the world, the rice-like dish is steamed and served as a side for meat and also can be a bed for vegetables or stew. In this chapter Linda Parelli spices up couscous with onion, pine nuts, fresh mint, lemon, olive oil and more.

Sides also can be based on whatever ingredients are abundant and easy to find in an area. Chuck-wagon cook Kent Rollins of Hollis, Okla., has experienced bumper crops of squash and had to find a variety of tasty ways to prepare it.

"You have to get creative making all type of dishes," he says. "It's sort of like Forrest Gump [and shrimp]–there's squash relish, squash bread, a squash cake and squash pickles. You can fry it, bake it, boil it, broil it, grill it. Heck, I've even tried to make ice cream with it."

Emily McCartney, Marianne and Todd's daughter, is only one of the R.A. Brown family members and ranch hands who has represented the outfit in Western Horseman *throughout the years.*

DARRELL DODDS

Barbequed Onions

Throw these on your grill for a colorful, tasty side to serve alongside your meat.

purple onions, ½ onion per person
barbeque sauce

Peel onions and quarter each, slicing three-fourths of the way down through each onion.
Do not cut completely through the onion.

Place each onion on a piece of aluminum foil large enough to cover onion completely.
Fill each onion half full of barbeque sauce. Seal foil around onion.

Place on grill alongside meat you might be cooking. Onions are most tender if cooked 1½ hours.

Marianne McCartney
Throckmorton, Texas

An R.A. Brown Ranch recipe featured in *Round-Up Cookin'* by the First Ladies of the
Texas Ranch Roundup Rodeo, 1990.

Bundles of Green Beans

*This is my go-to vegetable dish! People always like it, and it has become a favorite
frequently requested at family gatherings.*

3 cans whole green beans
about ½ package of uncooked bacon
⅓ cup brown sugar
⅓ cup butter or margarine, melted
dash of garlic salt
black pepper to taste

Preheat oven to 350 degrees.

Drain green beans. Divide into individual servings and wrap each serving with ½-slice uncooked bacon.
Place in a 9-by-13-inch baking dish and set aside.

Mix together brown sugar, butter and garlic salt, then pour over top of bundles. Sprinkle with black pepper.

Bake in 350-degree oven, uncovered for 30 minutes. Yield: 8 to 10 servings.

Tip: Here's another option for cooking the green bean bundles. Raise the oven rack and
place the bundles under broiler for just a short time. Watch closely so they don't burn!

Marianne McCartney
Throckmorton, Texas

From *Calf Fries to Caviar*, by Janel Franklin and Sue Vaughn, 1983.

75

Grilled Parmesan Zucchini

When your grill is hot, why not cook savory vegetables alongside your meat?

2 zucchini
3 tablespoons butter, softened
2 cloves garlic, minced
½ tablespoon parsley, chopped
½ tablespoon basil, chopped
½ cup grated Parmesan cheese

Preheat grill to medium-high heat and coat the grate with cooking spray
to prevent the zucchini from sticking.

Cut zucchini in half crosswise, and then slice each half into two or three slices lengthwise.
Mix butter, garlic, parsley and basil in a bowl, and spread the mixture on both sides of the zucchini slices.
Sprinkle Parmesan on the tops of each zucchini slice.

Place the zucchini slices on the grill, cheese side up, and grill until the cheese melts and
the slices are warm, tender and show grill marks, about 7 to 10 minutes.

Tip: Other vegetables cook easily on the grill, too. Try coating asparagus with olive oil and sprinkling with
garlic powder and kosher salt before grilling. Just remember to turn the asparagus every few minutes.

Jennifer Denison
Sedalia, Colorado

Roasted Veggies

*Slice and dice a favorite vegetable or combine several for a colorful and flavorful
side dish to complement any meal.*

Preheat oven to 350 degrees.

chopped vegetables of choice
cooking oil of choice, only a spoonful or two
seasonings of choice

Toss chopped vegetables with oil and seasonings. Spread in a single layer on a baking pan.

Roast at 350 degrees until browned—tender, but still crisp.

Tip: In addition to the typical peppers, onions, potatoes or zucchini, try roasting butternut squash,
broccoli, eggplant or even turnips. The secret to great roasted potatoes: Put them in cold water,
then drain and pat the potatoes dry before baking.

Patricia Wilson
Topeka, Kansas

Campfire Potatoes

The Rocking K Chuck Wagon's potato recipe is a perfect side dish for any meal, no matter if it's prepared in the great outdoors or in your kitchen.

3 pounds baking potatoes, washed and
   cut into ¼-inch cubes
1 red, 1 yellow and 1 green bell pepper,
   coarsely chopped
2 yellow onions, coarsely chopped
¼ cup olive oil

2 tablespoons flour
1 teaspoon garlic
salt and pepper to taste
1½ cups shredded Monterey Jack cheese
1½ cups heavy cream
3 tablespoons butter

Preheat oven to 400 degrees if using conventional oven.

Toss vegetables with oil, mixing thoroughly.
Sprinkle flour, garlic, salt, pepper, and cheese
over vegetables and toss again.

Coat a cast-iron skillet or a large, shallow
baking dish with oil. Spread potato mixture
evenly in the skillet or dish.

Pour heavy cream over the potato mixture,
and dot the top with butter.

Bake in an oven preheated to 400 degrees for
approximately 1 hour,
stirring after 30 minutes,
until the top is golden brown and
the potatoes are tender.

When cooking in a Dutch oven over a campfire,
put potatoes and other vegetables in a cast-iron
skillet with a small amount of oil. Cook on low
heat until the potatoes start to get tender.

Transfer the mixture to a Dutch oven
and stir in all remaining ingredients
except cream and butter.

Dot butter on top and pour cream over the
potato mixture.

Put on Dutch-oven lid and cook until done,
using coals on top of and under the Dutch oven.

Use a small amount of coals so that the
dish cooks slowly. Stir after 30 minutes,
and cook until the top is golden brown
and the potatoes are tender.

Jack and Karleen Boyd
Lubbock, Texas

JENNIFER DENISON

A chuck-wagon cook-off always proves entertaining for anyone who wants another perspective of the Old West, life on the trail or campfire cooking.

PAUL WEED

Roasted Pistachio Rice

Here's a favorite recipe served at the Double Horn Ranch table.

2 tablespoons olive oil
½ cup chopped yellow onion
¼ cup chopped red pepper
¼ cup chopped green pepper
1 carrot, finely chopped.
1 garlic clove, minced

2 tablespoons fresh, chopped cilantro
2 tablespoons butter
salt and pepper to taste
2 cups cooked brown or white rice
¾ cup toasted pistachio nuts.

Combine olive oil, onion, peppers and carrot in a pan. Sauté until onion is translucent.

Then add garlic, cilantro, butter, salt, pepper, rice and nuts.

Sauté for 3 minutes more before serving.

Dalene Cameron
Bluff Dale, Texas

Dalene and Craig Cameron enjoy life with horses and always try to make healthy food choices, no matter if they're on the road to the next clinic or at their ranch home.

JOHN BRASSEAUX

79

Creamed Veggies

Margaret Frank, my grandmother-in-law, passed along this family-friendly recipe that can be made from scratch or by using frozen vegetables.

Veggies

2 cups potatoes, cubed and cooked

2 cups carrots, sliced and cooked

2 cups peas, cooked

2 cups green beans, cooked

Prepare and cook vegetables. Set aside, but don't drain until cream sauce is prepared so vegetables remain warm until sauced and served.

Cream Sauce

3 cups hot milk

¼ cup margarine or butter

3 tablespoons cornstarch

salt and pepper to taste

In a saucepan, mix milk, butter and cornstarch. Heat and stir until thickened to desired consistency.

Drain and mix the potatoes, carrots, peas and green beans. Then pour the sauce over the vegetables. Stir well and salt and pepper to taste.

Tip: When time is short, use frozen vegetables and prepare according to package directions.

Katie Frank
Fort Worth, Texas

Garlic-Bouillon New Potatoes

One of my mother's favorite company-dinner side dishes—always a hit with family and friends and so easy to prepare ahead of time.

canned whole new potatoes, drained, enough to feed your dinner crowd

beef bouillon, enough to cover potatoes with room to spare

garlic powder or garlic salt to taste

black pepper to taste, optional

Prepare the potatoes several hours before your meal—the night before is even better. Drain canned potatoes and pour enough beef brother over the potatoes to cover, plus an inch or so more. Season broth and potatoes with garlic powder or garlic salt to taste. You can add black pepper now or let guests suit their own tastes at the table.

Cover potatoes and put in the refrigerator to marinate. The longer the potatoes marinate, the better the flavor. Before the meal, heat potatoes thoroughly over a low or medium-low burner.

Tip: This is a great make-ahead side dish to serve with ham, as well as with beef, and any leftover potatoes make a wonderful salad.

Fran Devereux Smith
Fort Worth, Texas

Roasted Okra with Pico de Gallo

You've never met okra fixed like this—not boiled or fried,
but baked and served with a flavorful topping.

Okra

25 fresh okra pods, sliced ⅓-inch thick
3 tablespoons olive oil
1 teaspoon kosher salt, or to taste
½ teaspoon black pepper, or to taste

Preheat oven to 425 degrees.

Arrange the okra slices in one layer on a foil-lined cookie sheet covered with cooking spray. Drizzle okra with olive oil and sprinkle with salt and pepper. Bake in the preheated oven for 10 to 15 minutes.

Pico de Gallo

3 small chopped tomatoes
¼ onion, finely chopped
1 or 2 finely chopped fresh jalapenos
¼ cup cilantro leaves, finely chopped
⅛ teaspoon salt
¼ teaspoon black pepper
1 small clove garlic, minced

Mix ingredients together and serve over the roasted okra.

Suzie Cox
Bloomfield, New Mexico

Suzie Cox really enjoyed the Western Horseman gathering in Amarillo, Texas, particularly the opportunity to spend the day riding with husband Tim.

JENNIFER DENISON

Minty Couscous

*Couscous, considered a staple in other parts of the world, is so good in this dish
that you could make a meal of it!*

1 pack plain, small grain couscous, or 4 cups
olive oil
1 medium onion
½ cup pine nuts
juice of one lemon
salt
pepper
1 cup or small bunch of fresh mint leaves

Using just enough hot or cold water to cover the grains,
soak the couscous in a bowl until it is soft—about 10 minutes.

In a pan, sauté onions in olive oil on medium-high heat until they start to brown and get a little crispy edge.
Add the pine nuts and allow them to brown with the onions for the last couple of minutes.

Turn down the temperature and add the couscous to the pan, stirring to combine well with onions
and pine nuts. Pour in the juice of half the lemon. Add salt and pepper, and stir thoroughly.
Cover pan with the lid and allow mixture to warm through for about 5 minutes.

Taste to check that lemon flavor and seasoning are as you prefer.
Chop the mint and add to the couscous just before serving.
Serve with lemon wedges and a sprig of mint.

Tip: Minty Couscous goes great with beef, chicken, sausage, and pork.

Linda Parelli
Pagosa Springs, Colorado

Refried Beans

This family recipe from my mother-in-law, Carrie Frank, can make any meal seem like home—no matter where we are.

15.5-ounce can pinto beans, rinsed and drained
3 tablespoons extra virgin olive oil
½ medium onion, chopped
4 cloves garlic
1 tablespoon ground coriander
½ teaspoon ground cumin

⅔ to 1 cup chicken broth (Homemade or low-sodium is fine.)
kosher salt
ground pepper
1 tablespoon fresh coriander, chopped
cilantro, optional

In a large bowl, mash two-thirds of the beans with a fork and set aside. Reserve the remainder of the beans.

In medium-sized skillet, warm oil over medium-high heat. Add onion and cook for 4 minutes or until brown. Add garlic and continue to cook until brown.
Next, add spices and cook 1 minute more until fragrant.

Add in the mashed beans and half of the broth. Cook and stir until thick, about 5 minutes.

Then add reserved beans and enough more of the broth to loosen up the mashed beans. Simmer until thick, about 2 minutes.

Season to taste with salt and pepper. Add fresh coriander and cilantro and serve.

Katie Frank
Fort Worth, Texas

Squash Casserole

What an easy fix! No need to measure anything; just slice up enough veggies to feed the crowd you're expecting for dinner.

yellow squash, sliced
zucchini squash, sliced
onion, chopped
tomatoes, sliced

bacon, cooked and broken up, or Real Bacon Bits
Spike seasoning
black pepper
cheddar cheese, shredded

Preheat oven to 350 degrees.

Layer each vegetable in a 9-by-13-inch backing dish and top with bacon.
Sprinkle with seasonings. Add cheese on top.

Cover and cook 30 to 35 minutes at 350 degrees. Yield: 8 to 10 servings.

Tip: The Spike seasoning can be a little difficult to find sometimes, but I highly recommend it on cooked vegetables and even cold sandwiches!

Marianne McCartney
Throckmorton, Texas

Green Beans and New Potatoes

In the summer, Sunday supper usually includes this dish as a side or main meal.
Most of the ingredients can be gathered fresh from the garden.

2 pounds fresh green beans, washed and snapped
1 pound bacon or salt pork, sliced into small pieces
8 red-skinned potatoes
½ white or yellow onion, diced
2 tablespoons garlic
salt and pepper to taste

Combine all ingredients in a slow-cooker or large pot, and fill with water till covered.
Cook on low in the slow-cooker for 3 hours or boil in the pot for 45 minutes,
until beans and potatoes are tender.

Jennifer Denison
Sedalia, Colorado

JENNIFER DENISON

85

Melitta's Sweet Potatoes

This recipe came from the late Melitta Bergen, a native Estonian and wife to Chan, who retired as editor after 25 years at **Western Horseman,** *which had followed his 21 years in the U.S. Army.*

Sweet Potatoes

½ cup sugar

1½ cups sweet potatoes, cooked and mashed

8-ounce package cream cheese

2 eggs

dash of salt

Preheat oven to 350 degrees.

Mix ingredients and put in 9-inch pan. Set aside while preparing topping.

Topping

1 cup chopped pecans

1 cup corn flakes, crushed

½ cup brown sugar

½ cup melted butter

Mix pecans, corn flakes and brown sugar and put on top of sweet potatoes. Drizzle ½ cup melted butter over the top. Bake 30 minutes in 350-degree oven.

Marsha Witte
Peyton, Colorado

Ranch-raised Marsha Witte and husband Randy, who retired as longtime **Western Horseman** *publisher, continue to raise cattle and enjoy horses on their Red Ink Ranch near Colorado Springs, Colorado.*

RANDY WITTE

January's Red Beans and Rice

Always a people-pleasing favorite—hearty and filling!

1 pound dried red beans, rinsed and sorted
3 tablespoons bacon grease
¼ cup chopped tasso or chopped ham
1½ cups chopped yellow onion
¾ cup chopped celery
¾ cup chopped green bell pepper
½ teaspoon black pepper
pinch of cayenne
3 bay leaves
1 tablespoon dried parsley

2 tablespoons fresh thyme
½ pound smoked sausage,
   cut in half lengthwise
   and sliced into 1-inch pieces
1 pound smoked ham hocks
3 tablespoons chopped garlic
10 cups chicken stock or water
½ teaspoon salt, or to taste
4 cups cooked rice
¼ cup green onions for garnish

Soak beans overnight.

In a large pot, heat bacon grease. Add tasso or chopped ham and cook for 1 minute.
Then add yellow onions, celery and bell pepper.
Season with black pepper and cayenne.
Cook until veggies are soft, 4 minutes or so.

Next, add bay leaves, parsley, thyme, sausage and ham hocks.
Brown for 4 minutes. Then add garlic and cook for another minute more.

Add beans and liquid to the pot.
Stir well and bring to boil.

Then reduce heat and simmer, uncovered, stirring occasionally until beans are tender and the broth starts to thicken, about 2 hours.

Then move pot of beans from heat. With the back of a heavy spoon, mash a fourth of the beans against the side of the pot.

Cook another 20 minutes until creamy.

Remove bay leaves and season with salt to taste.

Serve over cooked rice with green onions as garnish.

Tip: Some sausages might bring the amount of salt you desire to the dish, so you might not need to add any salt at all.

January Wiese
Dripping Springs, Texas

According to Cory Wiese, who handles Western Horseman's *digital media, wife January's red beans and rice are the best!*

GENE HYDER

87

Green Rice

This side-dish standard comes with options so you can use what's available in the pantry, rather than make a trip to the store.

boiling water
1 package chopped, frozen broccoli, or use fresh, chopped spinach
½ cup onion, chopped
½ stick oleo or margarine
½ cup chopped celery
1⅓ cup uncooked Minute® Rice
1 can cream of mushroom, chicken or celery soup—your preference
1 small jar Cheez Whiz

Preheat oven to 350 degrees.

Pour boiling water over frozen broccoli in a colander and set aside to drain.

In a small pan, sauté onion in oleo and add celery.

Then combine celery and onion with rice, soup, Cheez Whiz, and drained broccoli.

Place in a casserole dish and bake at 350 degrees for 40 minutes.

Nancy Hughes
Fort Worth, Texas

Sweet and Spicy Beans

Short on prep time and long on taste! All you need is time enough to bake this dish.

1 large can Ranch-Style Beans
1 can Ro*tel tomatoes
2 or 3 cloves garlic, minced
3 tablespoons brown sugar
1 bunch cilantro, chopped, optional

Preheat oven to 350 degrees.

Mix first four ingredients in casserole dish. Bake at 350 degrees for about 40 minutes.

If desired, add chopped cilantro and bake 10 minutes more.

Marianne McCartney
Throckmorton, Texas

JENNIFER DENISON

Hearty Hominy

*This home-style side dish is requested on the Withers Ranch Wagon,
which feeds spring branding crews there and at the neighboring outfits.*

1 pound bacon, diced

1 large onion, chopped

2 tablespoons minced garlic

2 6-pound cans white hominy, drained

2 4-ounce cans green chilies or jalapeños,
    depending on how spicy you want it

1 32-ounce container of sour cream

1 32-ounce bag grated cheddar or Monterey Jack cheese, or a mix of both

Fry bacon in a 12-inch Dutch oven until crispy. Remove bacon, and cook the onion and garlic in bacon grease. Once the onion is tender, add the hominy, cooked bacon and green chilies or jalapeños. Simmer until hot and the hominy has cooked down a little.

Remove from fire for about 10 minutes with the lid on the Dutch oven, and then stir in sour cream and cheese. Serves a branding crew of about 20 to 25.

Tina and Daryl Waite
Hugo, Colorado

89

JENNIFER DENISON

Sparklin' Potatoes

*Here's a different take on a traditional side dish—potatoes—
that's sure to please guests at your table.*

1 pound bacon, sliced
2 chopped onions
2 jalapeños, chopped
8 to 10 potatoes
Red River Ranch Seasoning to taste
½ to 1 tablespoon minced garlic
pepper, to taste
2 cans lemon-lime soda

If using a conventional oven, preheat to 350 degrees.

Brown bacon with jalapeños and onions, drain grease and set aside.

Wash and slice potatoes a ½-inch thick. Layer potatoes and bacon mixture,
ending with potatoes on top, in a Dutch oven or casserole dish.
Season with Red River Ranch Seasoning, garlic and pepper. Pour soda over mixture.

Cook in a Dutch oven, with coals on top and at bottom of oven.

If using a conventional oven, cover casserole dish and bake at 350 degrees for 20 to 30 minutes,
or until potatoes are tender.

Kent Rollins
Hollis, Oklahoma

From *A Taste of Cowboy* by Kent Rollins, © 2015 by Kent Rollins.
Reprinted by permission of Houghton Mifflin Harcourt Publishing Company. All rights reserved.

Jovonne's Beans

Pinto beans are a staple around many dinner tables, especially in New Mexico, and my mother's family recipe is a tried-and-true one.

4 cups pinto beans, picked and washed
¼ to ½ cup bacon grease, or 4 or 5 slices of salt pork ¼-inch-thick
salt to taste
10 cups water

Bring beans and water to a rolling boil for 1 minute. Remove from heat. Let stand for 1 hour.

Drain and rinse beans. Refill pot with fresh water and bring back to simmer.
Add ¼- to ½-cup bacon grease or sliced salt pork. Cook beans 4 to 5 hours.
Make sure to keep plenty of water in the pot to cover the beans and stir often.

Thirty minutes before serving, salt beans to taste and mash them a bit with a potato masher
for thicker juices. You must be extra vigilant not to scorch the beans from this point.
Serve with Aunt Jewel's Chowchow recipe in Chapter 2.

Suzie Cox
Bloomfield, New Mexico

Macaroni and Corn Casserole

An easy casserole to make and a satisfying alternative to the standard mac-and-cheese side dish.

1 stick butter, cut into slices
1 15 ¼-ounce can whole-kernel corn
1 15 ¼-ounce can cream-style corn
1 cup uncooked macaroni
1 cup Velveeta cheese, cubed

Preheat oven to 350 degrees.

Combine all ingredients in a casserole dish and bake at 350 degrees for 1 hour.

Pat Honey Mosher
La Junta, Colorado

Sweet Potato Puree

A delicious spin on mashed potatoes and a wonderful side dish for meats of all kinds!

2 to 4 sweet potato yams
½ to 1 cup sour cream

Peel the yams and cut into small cubes.

Steam cut-up potatoes until tender, about 12 to 15 minutes, checking frequently.

Mash sweet potatoes with sour cream. Add a little salt and pepper to taste before serving, but it doesn't need much.

Tip: This Sweet Potato Puree is great served under steak, pork or chicken.

Linda Parelli
Pagosa Springs, Colorado

COCO/FIREFLY FOTOS, COURTESY PARELLI NATURAL HORSEMANSHIP

Weather the Elements

An experienced chuck-wagon cook shares four tips for cooking over an open flame in less-than-ideal conditions.

Living and cooking off a chuck wagon in Arizona, Barbara Kennedy, owner of the Cowgirls Forever wagon, has prepared meals in wind and heat. She also has prepared meals at high elevations and in cooler climates. Here, she offers tips for cooking successfully in the elements.

1. Wind fans the flames, causing the coals to burn hotter and unevenly. Then, your Dutch oven heats faster, so you need to rotate the oven and lid more frequently, as well as check your moisture levels regularly to prevent burning your dish.

"Some [Dutch-oven] cooks dig a pit about 2 feet wide, 4 to 6 feet long and 18 inches deep, and build their fires in there to keep the fire out of the wind," Kennedy says. "Others carry a piece of sheet metal and use it as a wind break."

2. Heat and sun also contribute to a Dutch oven heating up quickly and cooking faster.

"Be sure to check the moisture inside the Dutch oven," Kennedy advises. "And rotate the Dutch oven or remove coals to keep it cooking evenly."

3. Cold ground absorbs heat from your coals, so it takes longer for the coals to heat and for a dish to cook. In this situation, some cooks place coals on top of a metal shield to keep the heat from going right into the ground.

"If it's cold, I just build a bigger fire and spread it out so it heats the ground," Kennedy says.

4. High altitude affects the rising of baked goods and also contributes to a Dutch oven requiring more time to cook a dish than is necessary at lower elevations. Kennedy says she just takes that into account when cooking at high elevations and allows more time for the food to get done.

—Jennifer Denison

PAUL WEED

Barbara Kennedy of the Cowgirls Forever Wagon team says steps can be taken to ensure tasty meals, even during bad weather.

PAUL WEED

BREADS 5

When feeding cowboys, if you can't bake bread, you're probably not considered a very good cook. On the chuck wagon in the 1880s, bread was served with every meal to sop up beans and gravy. If there was extra, a cowboy might wrap up a leftover piece of bread in oilcloth and put it in his saddlebag to eat later in the day. Bread continues to be a staple at the dinner table nowadays—to make sandwiches, top with gravy or smother with butter and jam.

Long ago, the type of bread made on the wagon varied by the ingredients readily available in a particular region. For example, on the Northern Plains wheat was plentiful, so breads commonly were made with wheat flour. For centuries in the Southwest, Native Americans harvested corn, then dried and ground it into cornmeal. Pioneers and chuck-wagon cooks learned to make a simple batter by combining cornmeal with eggs. Once baked over the fire, the cornbread became thin and dense, which made it filling, as well as easy to store and transport long distances.

There was also sourdough, which was not only used to make bread, but also to tan hides. The oldest type of leavened bread, sourdough had been discovered by ancient Egyptians and became popular during the California Gold Rush. Sourdough begins with a "starter," a mixture of flour and water left to ferment with wild yeasts in the air. Sourdough starters more than 100 years old still are being replenished and used. However, sourdough flavors can differ, based on where and how the starter was made, so sourdough from San Francisco, Calif., tastes differently than sourdough made in Fort Worth, Texas.

A chuck-wagon meal isn't complete without something made from sourdough, whether it's pancakes, biscuits, cinnamon rolls or some other bread. In this chapter, you find a simple sourdough starter that has been handed down for generations and used to make award-winning biscuits, plus other bread recipes, ranging from basic buns to beer bread, hearty cornbread and sweet breads. There are even a couple of spread recipes — ideal toppings for warm biscuits and rolls.

It doesn't matter what recipe you use, the aroma of homemade bread, fresh out of the oven, is nostalgic of a simpler time when everything was made from scratch, long before boxed mixes and electric bread-makers were used.

JENNIFER DENISON

Chuck-Wagon Yeast Rolls

Nothing says "loving" like hot yeast rolls from the oven!

1 stick butter
2 packages RapidRise™ Yeast
2 cups lukewarm water, 100 to 110 degrees
2 eggs, beaten
5 cups all-purpose flour
10 tablespoons sugar
1 teaspoon salt

Preheat oven to 425 degrees.

Melt butter and set aside.

Mix yeast with lukewarm water in a separate container and set aside.

In another bowl, beat eggs and set aside.

Combine flour, sugar and salt in a large mixing bowl.
Then pour yeast-and-water mixture and beaten eggs into dry ingredients. Mix well.

Turn dough out onto floured surface and knead for about 4 minutes.

Roll dough into balls and dip each in the melted margarine.
Place on a 9-by-13 cookie sheet in a warm area or a warm, but not hot, Dutch oven and cover with a towel.
Let the rolls rise for 30 minutes.

Bake at 425 degrees for 15 minutes or until golden brown. Pour remaining butter over rolls.

Teresa and Bobby Burleson
Weatherford, Texas

Cinnamon-Honey Butter

A great topping for a fresh biscuit or a slice of homemade bread!

¼ pound unsalted butter, room temperature
3 tablespoons honey
¼ teaspoon ground cinnamon
⅛ teaspoon kosher salt

Combine all ingredients in a bowl and blend until smooth. Spread on a homemade biscuit and enjoy!

Katie Frank
Fort Worth, Texas

Chocolate Zucchini Bread

Here's a new twist on an old standard—especially great to have when the garden produces well.

3 eggs
2 cups sugar
1 cup vegetable oil
1 teaspoon vanilla
2 squares, 1 ounce each, unsweetened
  baking chocolate
2 cups grated zucchini

3 cups flour
½ teaspoon baking powder
1 teaspoon salt
1 teaspoon baking soda
1 teaspoon cinnamon
1 cup coarsely chopped almonds, optional

Preheat oven to 350 degrees.

Beat eggs in a bowl until lemon-colored. Then beat in sugar and oil. Add vanilla and set aside.

Melt chocolate squares in a double-boiler. Stir into egg mixture and add zucchini.

In a separate bowl, sift flour with baking powder, salt, baking soda and cinnamon.
Then, with a large spoon, stir all into zucchini mixture, along with almonds, if desired.
When thoroughly mixed, spoon into two well-oiled 9-by-5 loaf pans.

Bake at 350 degrees for 1 hour, 20 minutes or until done.
Let bread cool in pans for 15 to 20 minutes.
Then turn out on a rack to cool. Serve bread when cool or even chilled.

Nancy Hughes
Fort Worth, Texas

Applesauce-Raisin Sweet Bread

A wonderful treat to have on hand when company's coming,
and that's easy to do because this loaf bread also freezes well.

1 egg, slightly beaten
1 cup applesauce
¼ cup butter, melted
¼ cup brown sugar, firmly packed
2 cups flour, sifted
2 teaspoons baking powder
¾ teaspoon salt

½ teaspoon baking soda
½ teaspoon cinnamon
1 teaspoon nutmeg
½ teaspoon ginger
½ cup raisins, soaked 1 hour in rum
¼ cup chopped pecans or walnuts

Preheat oven to 350 degrees.

In a bowl, combine egg, applesauce, butter and brown sugar. Mix well. Stir in flour, baking powder, salt, baking soda and spices until batter is smooth. Add drained raisins and nuts, and blend well.

Pour batter into well-greased loaf pan and bake at 350 degrees for about 1 hour.
Cool before removing from pan.

Tip: This sweet bread can be frozen for later use. I'm not really exactly sure about the original recipe as I've sometimes substituted with what was available through the years.

Carol Laramore Gipson
Eaton, Colorado

As adapted from *The Great Entertainer*, Buffalo Bill Historical Center, Roberts Rinehart, 2002.

Perhaps Western Horseman's *most recognizable faces, Charlene and Butch Morgan provided several recipes, shared with them by two women of the West —Butch's sister, Carol Laramore Gipson, and in-law Pat Honey Mosher.*

WALTER WORKMAN

JENNIFER DENISON

Humpy's Fried Cornmeal Bread

*Years ago "Humpy," the Hashknife cook on the Arizona ranch, gave this recipe to the late Stella Hughes, a longtime contributor to **Western Horseman.***

4 or 5 good handfuls of yellow cornmeal
egg-sized hunk of lard
2 pinches of salt
3 large pinches of sugar
boiling water

Mix all ingredients together and add enough boiling water to make a batter.
Fry like hot cakes. Goes well with beans or turnip greens.

From *Chuck Wagon Cookin'* by Stella Hughes. © 1974, The Arizona Board of Regents.
Reprinted by permission of the University of Arizona Press.

Rebeleven Strawberry Butter

The "Rebeleven" included the U.S. Air Force Academy cadets in my dad's Squadron 11 back in the 1970s, which is why my mother renamed the recipe originally given to her by another Air Force wife.

2 sticks of oleo or butter, softened
1 cup powdered sugar
1 10-ounce package frozen strawberries, thawed

Place the ingredients in a blender and combine well.
Store in a covered container in the refrigerator. Serve on toast or warm muffins.

Tip: This spread is especially good on hot bran muffins.

Christine Hamilton
Fort Worth, Texas

Mother's Banana Bread

There's no comfort food quite like warm banana bread with chocolate chips.

½ cup Crisco® or butter
1 cup of sugar
2 eggs
1 teaspoon vanilla
2 cups of flour
1 teaspoon soda, which isn't necessary with self-rising flour
2 large or 3 small bananas, mashed
½ cup chopped nuts or chocolate chips

Preheat oven to 350 degrees.

In a mixing bowl, cream Crisco and sugar together. Add eggs, vanilla and flour, with soda, if used, already sifted into the flour. Add bananas and nuts or chocolate. Stir well.

Pour batter into a lightly greased and floured loaf pan.

Bake at 350 degrees for almost an hour. Makes one regular loaf or four tea loaves.

Tip: Try the chocolate chips, instead of the nuts—or even both, and butter rather than Crisco. My mother, Malissa, adapted this recipe from one in an old cookbook from her home church in Albany, Georgia.

Christine Hamilton
Fort Worth, Texas

Basic White Buns

A favorite branding-day bread, the perfect complement to a savory barbecue.

2 cups hot water
1 tablespoon yeast
2 teaspoons salt
5 to 6 cups flour

Preheat oven to 350 degrees.

In a large bowl, dissolve yeast in hot water. Stir in salt. Gradually add flour, mixing well, until mixture forms a dough-like consistency. Shape dough into a ball and place in a large bowl coated with cooking spray. Cover dough with a towel and place in a warm area to rise.

When dough has doubled in size, which takes about 4 to 5 hours, knead well. Shape dough into 3-inch-diameter, 1-inch-thick disks and place on a greased cookie sheet, 2 inches apart.

Bake at 350 degrees for 25 to 30 minutes, until golden brown. Allow buns to cool, then slice in half, leaving a 1-inch tag to keep the halves attached. Yield: 10 buns

Karen and Jennifer Denison
Sedalia, Colorado

JENNIFER DENISON

Peach Cobbler Bread

Sweet, with a hint of spice, this fruity treat makes a nice breakfast or snack bread, or can be served as dessert.

Bread
⅓ cup butter
1 cup sugar
2 eggs
⅓ cup water
1 teaspoon vanilla extract
⅛ teaspoon almond extract
⅛ teaspoon rum extract
1 cup peeled, diced peaches
1 ¾ cups flour
2 teaspoons cinnamon
¼ teaspoon baking soda
½ teaspoon salt
1 teaspoon baking powder
½ cup chopped walnuts

Topping
2 tablespoons walnuts
2 tablespoons brown sugar

Preheat oven to 350 degrees.

Cream butter and sugar in a mixing bowl. Add the eggs, one at a time, beating well. Beat in water and extracts, and then stir in peaches.

In another bowl, combine flour, cinnamon, baking soda, salt and baking powder, and then gradually add the dry ingredients to the creamed mixture. Fold in walnuts. Pour batter into a greased, 9-by-5-by-3-inch loaf pan.

Combine topping ingredients and sprinkle over batter.

Bake at 350 degrees for 50 to 60 minutes or until a toothpick inserted near the center comes out clean. Cool 10 minutes before removing bread from pan.

Jennifer Denison
Sedalia, Colorado

JENNIFER DENISON

Daddy's Sourdough Biscuits

The C Bar C wagon shares its award-winning sourdough biscuit recipe, which was passed down to daughters Jean Cates and Sue Cunningham by Texan Dick Shepherd.

Sourdough Biscuits

yeast, about 1 teaspoon

4 cups sourdough starter from recipe at right

⅓ cup sugar

2 teaspoons salt

3 heaping teaspoons baking powder

12 tablespoons oil

3 ½ to 4 cups flour

melted butter, about 2 tablespoons

Preheat oven to 350 degrees if cooking biscuits in a conventional oven, rather than a Dutch oven on the campfire.

Sprinkle the yeast in the sourdough starter and stir. Add sugar, salt and baking powder, stirring between each ingredient. Add oil, stir, and then gradually sift in flour until the mixture reaches a doughy consistency.

Place dough onto a floured surface, and sprinkle flour on top. Flatten dough with your hand to desired thickness, and then cut out biscuits with a biscuit cutter.

Coat a 16-inch Dutch oven with nonstick cooking spray, and coat the bottom lightly with oil. Place biscuits in the oven, but avoid crowding them. Brush the biscuit tops with melted butter and let rise until wrinkles are gone.

Bake with coals under the Dutch oven and on the lid, or bake in a conventional oven preheated to 350 degrees, for 20 minutes or until done. Yield is about two dozen biscuits, depending on size and thickness.

Daddy's Sourdough Starter

Sourdough starter, a staple on every chuck wagon, can be made from Dick Shepherd's recipe the night before baking the biscuits.

4 cups warm water

1 package dry yeast

4 tablespoons sugar

4 cups flour

1 raw potato, peeled and cut into fourths

Dissolve yeast in warm water, stir well with wire whip, and let stand a few minutes.

Add sugar and stir until dissolved. Sift in flour, a small amount at a time, mixing well, until all flour is used. Add potato to the mixture.

Store the starter in a crock in a dry, warm area for 12 hours, stirring occasionally.

For every 2 cups of starter used, stir in 1 cup warm water, 1 cup flour and 1 tablespoon sugar to "feed" the starter.

Tip: Chuck-wagon cooks aren't known for precise measurements. The biscuit recipe calls "small amount" of yeast and melted butter. One teaspoon of yeast and two tablespoons of butter works well when preparing the recipe.

Jean Cates
Amarillo, Texas

Sue Cunningham
Harley, Texas

From *More Chuckwagon Recipes and Others,* by Jean Cates and Sue Cunningham, 1999.

Beer Bread

Who says making bread has to be a long, tedious job?

3 cups flour
⅓ cup sugar
4 tablespoons baking powder
1 teaspoon salt
1 can beer, room temperature
butter

Preheat oven to 350 degrees.

Mix flour, sugar, baking powder and salt. Add beer. Pour into a greased loaf pan or muffin pans.

Bake at 350 degrees for 55 minutes in loaf pan. When done, brush top with butter.

Jean Cates
Amarillo, Texas

Sue Cunningham
Harley, Texas

From *Chuckwagon Recipes and Others* by Jean Cates and Sue Cunningham, 1994.

Quick Sticky Buns

Quick and easy to make when unexpected guests arrive for coffee.

2 tablespoons butter
¼ cup brown sugar
¼ cup pancake syrup
¼ cup chopped nuts
1 teaspoon cinnamon
1 package, 10-count, refrigerator biscuits

Preheat oven according to biscuit instructions.

Combine first five ingredients—butter, sugar, pancake syrup, chopped nuts and cinnamon—together in a layer cake pan. Top with the biscuits.

Bake as package directs or until golden brown. Remove from oven and turn out onto plate. Serves 4.

Jean Cates
Amarillo, Texas

Sue Cunningham
Harley, Texas

From *Chuckwagon Recipes and Others* by Jean Cates and Sue Cunningham, 1994.

Through the years, Sue Cunningham and Jean Cates, along with their family members, who make up the C Bar C team, have claimed just about every major chuck-wagon cook-off title possible.

JENNIFER DENISON

109

Indian Fry Bread

Here's how this Southwestern staple has been prepared on one Arizona outfit's wagon.

2 tablespoons yeast
¼ cup sugar
2 cups warm water
¼ cup oil
1 teaspoon salt
5 cups flour
oil for frying

Soak the yeast and sugar in 2 cups of warm water until it foams on top, about 10 minutes. In a large bowl, preferably stainless steel, blend the yeast mixture with the oil and salt. Be sure the oil is not very cold.

Sift the flour a cup at a time into the mixture and work in with a pastry blender. After the third cup, mix in the rest of the flour by hand, adding enough to make a ball that is silky in texture and doesn't stick to your hands. Cover dough and allow it to rise in the bowl until double in size, about half an hour.

Remove dough from bowl and knead for 5 to 10 minutes, until no bubbles form.
Break off into golf-ball-sized balls and flatten with your palm.

Heat oil until a drop of water sizzles in it, then deep-fry dough rounds, searing both sides quickly and continuing to cook until browned. Remove fry bread from pan and drain.
Place in a Dutch oven and keep warm in the oven until ready to eat.

Joe St. Clair
Seligman, Arizona

From *Cow Country Cooking: Recipes and Tales From Northern Arizona's Historic Ranches*
by Kathy McCraine, Kathy McCraine Publisher, 2010.

KATHY MCCRAINE

Sour Cream Coffee Cake

Deliciously perfect to serve for brunch or a morning coffee break!

1 cup butter, softened
2 cups sugar
2 eggs
1 cup sour cream
½ teaspoon vanilla or almond extract
2 cups flour, sifted
1 teaspoon baking powder
¼ teaspoon salt
4 teaspoons sugar
1 cup chopped pecans or walnuts
1 teaspoon cinnamon

Preheat oven to 350 degrees.

Cream butter and 2 cups sugar. Beat until fluffy. Add eggs, one at the time, beating thoroughly when each egg is added. Then fold in sour cream and vanilla or almond extract. Set aside.

In a separate bowl, combine flour, baking powder and salt. Then fold into batter above.

In another container, combine 4 teaspoons sugar, nuts and cinnamon.

Place a third of the batter in a well-greased and floured Bundt pan. Sprinkle with ¾ cup of the nut mixture. Spoon on the remaining batter and top with the rest of the nut mixture.

Bake at 350 degrees for 1 hour. Then cool on a rack. Sift powdered sugar on top if desired.

Carol Laramore Gipson
Eaton, Colorado

As adapted from *The Great Entertainer*, Buffalo Bill Historical Center, Roberts Rinehart, 2002.

Chuck-wagon cook Kent Rollins, shown with wife Shannon and "Bonehead," has contributed greatly to Western Horseman's food column in recent years and has become a favorite with the readers.

JENNIFER DENISON

Mexican Cornbread

Surprise your branding crew with this recipe for cornbread with a kick.

½ pound chorizo or spicy sausage, chopped
2 tablespoons butter
1 cup sweet mini-peppers, diced
1 small yellow onion, chopped
2 cups Aunt Jemima® Self-Rising Yellow Corn Meal Mix
1½ cups milk

3 tablespoons vegetable oil
2 tablespoons sugar
1 egg, beaten
1 4-ounce can green chilies
1 ½ to 2 cups shredded cheddar cheese

Preheat oven to 425 degrees.

In a heated skillet, fry chorizo or sausage until cooked throughout, and then set aside.

In a separate skillet, melt butter and sauté peppers and onion approximately 10 minutes, or until tender.

In a mixing bowl, combine corn meal and milk. Stir in oil, sugar and egg until mixed thoroughly.
Add green chilies, and then slowly add the sausage and pepper mixture.

Pour half the cornmeal mixture into a greased Dutch oven, cast-iron skillet or cake pan.
Sprinkle the top with approximately 1½ cups shredded cheese, or until covered.
Pour the remaining cornmeal mixture over the cheese.

Bake at 425 degrees for 20 to 25 minutes, or until golden brown and a toothpick
inserted into the cornbread comes out clean.

Tip: This dish is very versatile. You can substitute bell peppers for the sweet peppers, and corn and yellow
hominy are great additions. I don't want to get too spicy on ya'll, but I like it with diced jalapeños.

Kent Rollins
Hollis, Oklahoma

ROSS HECOX

"Death" Bread

My family—always in a joking way—calls this recipe by that name because the bread is so deliciously unhealthy!

½ cup butter, room temperature

1 cup mayonnaise

¼ cup green onion, diced

1 teaspoon minced garlic

1 cup asiago cheese

1 cup Monterey Jack cheese

1 loaf French bread, sliced

Western Horseman *Associate Editor Katie Frank brings a strong background in the horse industry, particularly in equine health care, to the outfit.*

ROSS HECOX

Preheat oven to 350 degrees.

Mix all the ingredients, except the bread, in a bowl until well-blended.

Then spread mixture on top of bread slices and place in a baking pan or on a cookie sheet.

Bake at 350 degrees for about 7 minutes.

Then broil until golden brown and serve.

Katie Frank
Fort Worth, Texas

Uncle Charles' Cornbread

This longtime family recipe can be pepped up with Hatch chilies.

2 eggs

1 cup sour cream

1 cup cream-style corn

½ cup corn oil

1 cup corn meal

1½ teaspoon salt

3 teaspoons baking powder

Omit baking powder and salt if self-rising meal is used.

Preheat oven to 400 degrees.

Mix all ingredients well and
pour into an 8-inch Pyrex dish.

Bake at 400 degrees until golden brown,
about 30 minutes.

Cut into squares and serve hot or
allow to cool and freeze for later use.

Tip: My mother, Malissa, always made
this southern-style family recipe in a well-
seasoned iron skillet. After living out west,
she learned to add fresh, roasted Hatch
chilies, grown in New Mexico, on top
if she could get them.

Christine Hamilton
Fort Worth, Texas

*Longtime equine journalist Christine Hamilton moved from
Colorado to Texas to become editor of Western Horseman.*

ROSS HECOX

Wagon Restoration

*Neighboring ranchers traditionally help one another work cattle; having a wagon
to feed the crew helps ensure that such customs continue. It's the cowboy way.*

Daryl and Tina Waite manage Withers Ranch, located 10 miles south of Hugo, Colorado. Established in 1948 by Lawrence Withers, the ranch runs about 800 cows, all branded with the reverse ZD brand. The Withers Ranch wagon, restored by the Waites, is a working wagon used primarily to feed crews at spring brandings held at the ranch or on neighboring outfits. The Waites also take the wagon to nearby cowboy gatherings and cooking competitions.

In May of 2008, the Waites bought an old wagon made by Northwestern Manufacturing Company in Fort Atkinson, Wisc., which was in business from 1866 until the late 1930s. The couple stripped the paint and took the wagon apart to restore it as closely as possible to its original appearance. Restoring the wagon came with several obstacles.

"The most difficult was probably trying to get all the green enamel paint scraped off," Tina says. "The other hard thing was that we could find only one picture of a Northwestern wagon. It was difficult to replicate the striping and design with only a single picture, but I think we came really close."

Tina painted the wagon with milk paint and, with Daryl's help, rebuilt the sideboards. They found old-style nails and hardware in the scrap pile at the ranch and ordered some from Tom and Cheryle Elliott of Bar E Ranch in Clinton, Arkansas. The brake parts came from Wayne's Wagon Works in Angleton, Texas.

The couple also ordered a fly and found poles for it. Hansen Wheel and Wagon Shop in Letcher, S.D., built new wheels for the wagon.

"The chuck box has no drawers, other than little ones on the bottom, so we use ammo boxes, apple boxes and horseshoe-nail boxes," Tina explains.

The pantry behind the chuck box was found in an old shed on the ranch and predates 1948, when the ranch was owned by L. Jergens. The couple's oldest son, Chance, had remembered seeing the pantry in the shed.

"It [the wagon] feels like it is a part of all of us who still like to do things the cowboy way, keeping tradition alive," Tina says. "There is a group of people and neighbors that we always trade with for branding help, and this wagon has really pulled everyone together. It's our way of preserving what we see as a dying part of history, and it's important for us to raise our families knowing what is important and knowing where you come from and who you can count on."

—Jennifer Denison

A wagon enthusiast loves nothing more than finding realistic gear and equipment befitting the wagon.

JENNIFER DENISON

DESSERTS 6

Most cowboys have a sweet tooth, especially at the end of a meal, and there's no better way to satisfy that craving than by serving a decadent dessert. That doesn't mean a flowing fountain of chocolate or flaming crème brulée. In the past, cowboys who rode out with the wagon didn't have a lot of modern conveniences, such as reliable refrigeration, so milk and eggs weren't usually an option. But a good chuck-wagon cook occasionally made a simple cookie with nonperishable ingredients, such as flour, dried fruit and molasses, and that was a real treat. Today's chuck-wagon cooks make layer cakes, brownies, cobblers and other desserts in Dutch ovens over an open fire, which always seems to make them taste better.

In this section, we've rounded up a variety of dessert recipes for cakes, cobblers, cookies and more that can be made in a Dutch oven over the coals or in a baking dish and conventional oven. Some of the desserts sound fancy enough to be served in a five-star restaurant, such as Margarita Pie with Pretzel Crust, Jalapeño Cheesecake and Bread Pudding with Cherry Tequila Sauce. However, all of the recipes are quick and easy to make. Better yet, they use ingredients commonly found in most people's pantries (or liquor cabinets), which is important to those who can't run to the grocery in a short period of time.

Dessert isn't complete without a tin cup of slow-brewed cowboy coffee, and we've included a recipe for that, too. Cowboys are usually up and saddled before dawn, and a cup of strong coffee gives them the jolt they need to start their day.

Like a coffee-shop barista, even now each chuck-wagon cook has his own brewing technique. Learn more about the sock in the pot on the last page of this chapter. But, as one cookie points out, you never really know whose foot might have been in that old sock thrown in the coffeepot. Knowing cowboys, that sock might not have been washed.

That sock is why some cooks play it safe and prefer to place the grounds loose in the bottom of the pot. However, the grounds must settle before the coffee is poured. Adding a raw egg to a boiling pot of coffee and gently stirring it—without breaking the yolk—while the coffee simmers is another technique used to settle the grounds in the pot. But whatever method you prefer, there really isn't a bad cup of cowboy coffee, even down to the last drop in the pot.

JENNIFER DENISON

Apple Berry Crisp with Bourbon Sauce

Guests at The Home Ranch experience scenic horseback adventures and five-star cuisine, including such desserts as this fruity treat.

Crisp

10 large, tart, green apples
½ pint blackberries, raspberries or cranberries
2 tablespoons lemon juice
1¼ cups all-purpose or bread flour
¾ cup granulated sugar
¾ cup dark brown sugar
12 tablespoons, or 1 ½ sticks, cold unsalted butter

Preheat oven to 375 degrees.

Peel the apples, cut in half and remove the cores. Cut each apple half into 12 pieces.
Place apple pieces in lemon juice, and then spread them in a 2 ½-quart, shallow, earthenware baking dish.
Add the fresh berries on top of the apples and lightly press the fruit into the dish.

Combine flour and sugars with an electric mixer on low speed, using the paddle attachment.
Cut the butter into 18 pieces and add it while mixing. Continue mixing until mixture forms clumps,
then sprinkle the mixture over the fruit.

Bake approximately 40 minutes, or until the apples are tender and the topping is lightly browned.

Bourbon Sauce

2 large eggs
½ cup sugar
1/3 cup lemon juice
zest of one lemon
4 tablespoons unsalted butter
¾ cup bourbon
2 cups whipping cream

To prepare the bourbon sauce, whisk eggs and sugar
until double in volume and pale yellow in color. Add lemon juice and zest.

Cook in a double-boiler over high heat until thick. Stir with a whisk to let eggs cook evenly,
20 to 30 minutes.

Remove from heat. Cut in the butter, piece by piece, stirring until melted, and then add bourbon.

Top the crisp with the sauce and whipped cream when serving.

Clyde Nelson
Clarke, Colorado

Twice-as-Nice Chocolate Pie

*Twice as nice because the crowning glory for this tasty dessert can be either
a whipped-cream or a meringue topping.*

Pie
1 ready-made pie shell
1 cup sugar
3 tablespoons Hershey'®s cocoa
¼ tsp salt
3 tablespoons all-purpose flour
2 egg yolks (Save whites for meringue.)
2 tablespoons margarine
1¾ cups milk
1½ teaspoons vanilla flavoring

Bake pie shell according to directions. Cool completely.

Combine all pie-filling ingredients in a saucepan.
Stir well until all lumps are gone.
Cook over medium heat, stirring constantly until thick.

Pour filling into baked pie shell. Cool completely.
Add topping of your choice—whipped cream or meringue.

Whipped-Cream Topping
1 small container of whipping cream
1 teaspoon of sugar

Beat small container of whipping cream until thick. Add 1 teaspoon of sugar and spread on top of pie.

Meringue Topping
2 egg whites, reserved from pie filling
1 teaspoon of sugar

Preheat oven to 350 degrees.

Beat two egg whites and 1 teaspoon of sugar until stiff peaks form.
Spread on top of pie and bake at 350 degrees until lightly brown.

Madge King
Jackson, Mississippi

Grandmommy's Oatmeal Cookies

This family favorite gets especially high marks from **Western Horseman** *General Manager Ernie King.*

1¼ cups, or 2½ sticks, of margarine or butter-flavored shortening
¾ cup packed light brown sugar
½ cup sugar
1 egg
1 tablespoon vanilla flavoring
1 ½ cups all-purpose flour
1 teaspoon baking soda
1 teaspoon salt
3 cups quick oatmeal
1 cup chopped pecans

Preheat oven to 375.

Beat margarine, or shortening, and sugars until fluffy. Then add egg and vanilla.
Beat until well-incorporated.

In separate bowl, sift flour, soda and salt. Add flour mixture to sugar mixture, combining well.
Stir in oatmeal and pecans. Drop by rounded tablespoons onto ungreased cookie sheet.

Bake 8 to 9 minutes for a chewy cookie, 10 to 11 minutes for a crisp cookie. Makes 4½ dozen.

Madge King
Jackson, Mississippi

Around the office, Ernie King is known to appreciate culinary treats of all persuasions, particularly sweet ones, but those that come from his mother's kitchen top the list.

JENNIFER DENISON

121

Bread Pudding
with Cherry Tequila Sauce

*Western artist Mike Capron suggested that this recipe, originally made with a whiskey sauce,
be changed for West Texas cowboys who prefer the nectar of the agave.
The recipe serves about 30 average folks or 12 hungry cowboys.*

Bread

You can get by with any kind of bread
one or two days old.
Chef Emeril Lagasse says not to use sourdough,
but I think it's fine.

For our award-winning dessert, try the recipe below
for baking-powder biscuits.
Prepare them in a Dutch oven a day or two days
before you make the dessert.

Baking-Powder Biscuits

3 cups unbleached flour
2 tablespoons baking powder
1 teaspoon salt
¼ cup lard or butter
1 cup milk
vanilla to taste

If not baking in a Dutch oven
over the coals, preheat conventional oven to
about 400 degrees.

Sift the dry ingredients together,
and then cut in the lard or butter.
Add milk and vanilla slowly,
mixing with a wooden spoon or your hands
until the mixture forms a dough.

On a flour-dusted surface,
roll or pat the dough to about ⅝-inch thick.

Cut dough into 2-inch rounds
with a biscuit cutter. Place biscuits in a lightly
greased and floured pan or a Dutch oven,
with the edges touching each other.

Bake in a hot Dutch or conventional oven—about
400 degrees—until the biscuits are
a light golden brown.
Set aside for later use in bread pudding.

Spiced Tequila Cherries

1 cup coarsely chopped dried or
fresh cherries with pits removed
½ to 1 cup 100-percent agave tequila
1 cup sugar
½ teaspoon freshly ground cloves
½ teaspoon nutmeg

The night before serving the bread pudding
put the cherries in a pot with a mixture
of the tequila, sugar, cloves and nutmeg.
Simmer over a low fire for 1 hour or so,
and let them soak overnight.

Strain the cherries for use in the pudding recipe.
Reserve the remaining liquid to use in the sauce.

Pudding

1 dozen eggs, plus four or five
additional yolks
⅓ cup melted butter
2 tablespoons vanilla
4 cups sugar, or 3 cups if using evaporated milk
3 cups milk or 2 cans evaporated milk
1 cup spiced tequila cherries,
as prepared above and strained
1 cup crushed pecans
bread to cover the bottom of the pan

Preheat oven to 350 degrees.

Beat the eggs, and then add melted butter
and vanilla. Stir in sugar until dissolved,
and then add milk.

Coat the bottom and sides of a 14-inch Dutch
oven with butter, and cover the bottom about 1
inch deep with bread. Pour the pudding mixture
over the bread. Sprinkle pecans and strained
cherries on top and press into the mixture.

Bake at 350 degrees for about 30 minutes or until the top forms a crust.

Cherry Tequila Sauce

1 cup heavy cream
¼ cup butter
1 cup sugar
½ cup tequila or to taste
reserved liquid from cooking spiced cherries

Near serving time, combine cream, butter, sugar and tequila, and bring to a boil for a few minutes.

Then combine with the reserved liquid from the Spiced Tequila Cherries.

Pour the sauce over the entire pudding, or leave it on the side for individual servings.

This recipe serves about 30 average folks or 12 hungry cowboys.

Kit Haddock
Monument, Colorado

JENNIFER DENISON

Raisin Pie

My mom, Jovonne, passed along this recipe, and it's my husband's favorite!

Pie Crust
Preheat oven to 400 degrees. Pierce and bake your pie shell.

Raisin Filling
6 tablespoons flour

1 cup sugar

2 cups milk

3 egg yolks (Save whites for meringue.)

pinch of salt

2 tablespoons butter

1 teaspoon vanilla

1 cup soft raisins

In a 2-quart pan, mix dry ingredients, then add the rest—except the raisins—and mix well.

Place pan on medium heat and cook until mixture starts to thicken. Add raisins. Cook until thick. Remove from heat and set aside to cool.

Meringue
3 egg whites (Room temperature is best.)

¼ teaspoon cream of tartar

3 tablespoons sugar

1 teaspoon vanilla

Beat egg whites and cream of tartar until stiff. Slowly add sugar, then vanilla, while continuing to beat for approximately 1 minute more.

Put cooled raisin filling mixture into prepared pie shell and top with meringue.

Bake in 400 degree oven until meringue is browned to your preference. Check frequently.

Suzie Cox
Bloomfield, New Mexico

Orange Chocolate Chippers

Not your typical chocolate-chip cookies, but these always get rave reviews!

1 cup shortening

1 cup sugar

1 3-ounce package cream cheese

2 eggs

2 tablespoons grated orange peel

2 teaspoons vanilla

2 cups sifted flour

1 teaspoon salt

1 6-ounce package chocolate chips

Preheat oven to 350 degrees.

Cream together shortening, sugar and cream cheese. Add eggs, orange peel and vanilla; beat well.

Sift together flour and salt. Then add to creamed mixture, stirring well. Stir in chocolate chips. Using a teaspoon, drop dough 2 inches apart on a lightly greased cookie sheet.

Bake in 350-degree oven 12 minutes or until very lightly browned around the edges. Makes 4 dozen cookies.

Susan Morrison
Fort Worth, Texas

Drunk Pineapple Rum Cake

Celebrate a special day with this festive, fruity dessert. A little slice goes a long way.

2 cups sugar
2 sticks butter
4 eggs
3 cups flour
½ teaspoon baking soda

1 cup milk
½ teaspoon vanilla extract
2 teaspoons rum extract
1 8-ounce can pineapple rings
1½ cups coconut rum

Preheat oven to 350 degrees.

In a large mixing bowl, cream together sugar and butter. Beat in eggs, one at a time. Slowly beat in flour and soda, and then milk and extracts until all ingredients are well-blended.

Pour batter into a greased and lightly floured 11-by-13-inch cake pan, or into two 8- or 9-inch cake pans. Bake for about 40 minutes or until a toothpick inserted into the cake pulls out clean.

While the cake is baking, place pineapple rings on a plate or pan with edges.
Pour coconut rum over the rings until they are about halfway covered.
Depending on the size of the plate or pan, you might need to use more or less coconut rum.
Let the pineapple soak for at least 20 minutes, flipping the rings halfway through at 10 minutes.

Allow the cake to cool completely, and then remove it from the pan.
Top the cake with as many of the spiked pineapple rings as you wish.

Tip: For a smoky flavor, you can grill the pineapples before placing them on the cake.

Kent Rollins
Hollis, Oklahoma

From *A Taste of Cowboy* by Kent Rollins, ©2015 by Kent Rollins.
Reprinted by permission of Houghton Mifflin Harcourt Publishing Company. All rights reserved.

ROSS HICOX

Jalapeño Cheesecake

Inspired by a favorite Perini Ranch Steakhouse dessert originated by Tom Perini, this recipe melds sweet and spicy flavors with rich cream cheese.

Crust
2 cups graham cracker crumbs
½ cup pecan pieces
¼ cup sugar
½ cup melted butter

Combine dry ingredients and then add butter.
Mix until crumb mixture is moist and packs firmly.

Press crumb mixture into the bottom and halfway up
the sides of a spring-form pan.

Filling
3 8-ounce blocks cream cheese
   at room temperature
¾ cup sugar
1 teaspoon vanilla
3 eggs
1 to 2 fresh jalapeños, seeded
   and finely chopped

Preheat oven to 350 degrees.

Beat together cream cheese, sugar and vanilla.
When smooth, add eggs and jalapeños and mix
thoroughly. Pour batter into crumb-lined pan
and smooth top with a spatula.

Bake for 1 hour. Cheesecake will have shallow cracks.
Glaze cheesecake while still warm and then cook
additionally as described in the glaze recipe.

Glaze
¾ cup sour cream
3 tablespoons sugar
1 tablespoon lemon juice

Mix all ingredients and pour over warm
cheesecake in a smooth, even layer.

Bake 15 to 25 minutes until set.
Let cheesecake cool at room temperature,
and then refrigerate overnight.

Jalapeño Sauce
5 cups sugar
¾ cup bell pepper, seeded
   and finely chopped
¾ cup poblano pepper, seeded
   and finely chopped
¼ cup jalapeño, seeded and finely chopped
1 ½ cups vinegar
1 envelope fruit pectin

In a medium saucepan and over low heat, mix
sugar, peppers and vinegar. Stirring constantly,
bring mixture to a rolling boil.

Remove mixture from heat and stir in pectin.
Pour sauce into serving dishes or jars
and refrigerate.

Serve individual pieces of cheesecake
with pepper sauce drizzled over the top.

Tip: Tom Perini recommends using leftover sauce
on brisket, venison, chicken or lamb.

Ryan Sankey
McLeod, Montana, and Saint Jo, Texas

As inspired by and adapted from Tom Perini's
recipe in *Texas Cowboy Cooking*
by Tom Perini, Comanche Moon Publishing and
Perini Ranch, 2000.

JENNIFER DENISON

Mexican Lime Bars

*The sweet and tangy taste
of this dessert is refreshing
on a hot summer day.*

Crust

2 cups flour
½ cup powdered sugar
1 cup butter
½ teaspoon salt

Preheat oven to 350 degrees.

Combine crust ingredients and
blend with a fork.
Press mixture into a greased,
9-by-13-inch baking dish.

Bake for 20 to 25 minutes
or until lightly browned.

Topping

4 eggs
⅓ cup fresh lime juice
¼ cup flour
2 cups sugar
1 tablespoon grated lime zest
½ teaspoon baking powder
1 drop of green food coloring, optional
1 cup powdered sugar

Beat eggs and lime juice.
Stir in flour, sugar, zest and baking powder.
Add food coloring if desired.
Mix well, pour over baked crust and allow
dessert to chill until set.

Sprinkle with powdered sugar before cutting
into bars and serving.

Robert Boyd
Trent, Texas

JENNIFER DENISON

Shaker Sugar Pie

The Golden Lamb Inn, the oldest hotel in Ohio, made this dessert famous in the early 1800s and it's popular nowadays on the Bar E Ranch wagon.

1 9-inch unbaked pie shell, or make your own
1 cup brown sugar
½ cup flour
½ cup half-and-half cream
1 teaspoon vanilla
½ stick butter
nutmeg

Preheat oven to 350 degrees.

Thoroughly mix flour and brown sugar. Spread evenly in the bottom of the unbaked pie shell.

Mix half-and-half with vanilla, and pour over sugar mixture.

Slice butter into 12 pieces and distribute evenly over top of pie. Sprinkle with nutmeg.

Bake for 40 to 45 minutes, or until firm.

Cheryle and Tom Elliott
Clinton, Arkansas

From the *Bar E Ranch Chuckwagon Cookbook*, Bar E Ranch.

JENNIFER DENISON

Best-of-Show Brownies

Nothing beats a warm brownie fresh from the oven,
especially when the recipe is a tried-and-true favorite.

2 eggs
1 cup sugar
½ cup butter
1 square bitter Baker's chocolate
1 square semi-sweet Baker's chocolate
¾ cup all-purpose flour
½ teaspoon salt
1 cup chopped pecans
1 teaspoon vanilla

Preheat oven to 325 degrees.

Beat eggs slightly; add sugar and stir well.

In a separate container, melt butter and chocolate squares. Add to the egg mixture, stirring well.

In another bowl, mix flour, salt and pecans; then add to egg mixture.
Add vanilla to the batter and stir until well-blended. Do not beat!

Pour batter into a buttered 9-inch pan. Bake for 25 to 35 minutes.

Don Baskins
Tucumcari, New Mexico

Mayonnaise Cake

Handed down from one Air Force wife to another, including my mother,
this cake always proves to be a hit with the servicemen.

2 cups flour
1 cup sugar
3 tablespoons cocoa
1 teaspoon baking soda
1 teaspoon baking powder
1 cup cold black coffee
1 cup mayonnaise
1 teaspoon vanilla

Preheat oven to 350 degrees.

In a mixing bowl, combine all ingredients and blend well.

Pour into a lightly greased and floured 9-by-13 baking pan.

Bake for 30 to 35 minutes. When cool, ice with vanilla butter frosting, if desired.

Christine Hamilton
Fort Worth, Texas

129

Grandma's Oatmeal Cake

The brown sugar and pecan topping makes this dessert a real treat!

Oatmeal Cake

1½ cups quick-cooking oats
1¼ cups boiling water
1 cup sugar
1 cup brown sugar, packed
½ cup butter, softened
1 teaspoon vanilla
3 eggs
½ teaspoon salt
1 teaspoon baking soda
½ teaspoon baking powder
1 ½ cups all-purpose flour

Preheat oven to 350 degrees.

Combine rolled oats and boiling water in a bowl. Set aside and let sit.

In a separate bowl, combine both sugars and butter. Beat until well-mixed.
Add vanilla and eggs. Mix well.
Add prepared oatmeal and the remaining ingredients and mix well again.

Pour batter into a greased and floured 13-by-9-inch pan.

Bake at 350 for 35 to 45 minutes or until a toothpick inserted in the middle comes out clean.
Add topping before cake cools.

Cake Topping

¼ cup melted butter
⅔ cup packed brown sugar
¼ cup whipping cream
1 cup chopped pecans

Combine butter, brown sugar and whipping cream. Beat at high speed until smooth. Then stir in pecans.

Pour topping over warm cake and spread.

Turn oven on broil setting and place cake in oven for 1 to 2 minutes until topping is bubbly and light brown.
Cool before serving.

Teresa and Bobby Burleson
Weatherford, Texas

Margarita Pie with Pretzel Crust

This tangy, tantalizing dessert is a favorite at a historic Southwestern inn.

Pretzel Crust

1½ cups finely chopped pretzels
1 cup sugar
½ cup (1 stick) butter, melted

For the crust, pulse the pretzels and sugar in a food processor several times to combine.
Add the butter in a steady stream and process until mixed well. Press crushed pretzel mix over the bottom
and up the side of a 9-inch pie plate coated with nonstick cooking spray.

Tip: Do not use fat-free or low-fat pretzels in the crust, as the crust will not hold together when you cut it.
You can substitute graham crackers for the pretzels.

Margarita Pie

½ cup fresh lime juice
1 14-ounce can sweetened condensed milk
2 tablespoons gold tequila
2 tablespoons triple sec
2 cups heavy whipping cream, whipped
green food coloring, optional

For the pie, combine the lime juice,
condensed milk, tequila and triple sec in
a bowl and mix well.
Fold in the whipped cream.
Tint with green food coloring if you
desire a deeper color.

Spoon filling into the pretzel crust.
Cover with plastic wrap and freeze for
4 hours or up to a week.

To serve, garnish with additional
whipped cream and lime slices.
Serves six to eight.

Rancho De La Osa Guest Ranch
Sasabe, Arizona

From: *Tastes and Treasures: A
Storytelling Cookbook of Historic
Arizona*, The Historical League, 2007.

JENNIFER DENISON

Punk's Buttermilk Pie

Here's a family favorite, and the crust is easy, thanks to a food processor.

All-Butter Pie Crust

1¼ cups all-purpose flour

¼ teaspoon salt

10 tablespoons unsalted butter, chilled and cut into ½-inch pieces

2 to 5 tablespoons ice water

In a food processor, briefly pulse together the flour and salt. Add butter and pulse, using three to five 1-second pulses, until mixture forms chickpea-size pieces.
Add ice water 1 tablespoon at a time, and pulse until mixture is just moist enough to hold together.

Form dough into a ball, wrap in plastic and flatten. Refrigerate at least 1 hour before rolling out and baking pie.

Tip: This recipe yields a 9-inch crust and can be doubled for a double-crusted pie. Simply divide dough into two balls and flatten before chilling.

Buttermilk Pie Filling

3 eggs, beaten

½ cup butter, softened

2 cups sugar

3 rounded tablespoons flour

1 cup buttermilk

1 teaspoon vanilla

dash of nutmeg

1 9-inch unbaked All-Butter Pie Crust

Preheat oven to 350 degrees.

Beat eggs until frothy. Add butter, sugar and flour, and beat until smooth.

Stir in buttermilk, vanilla, and nutmeg.

Pour into pie shell.
Bake at 350 degrees for 40 to 60 minutes, or until center is firm.

January and Cory Wiese
Dripping Springs, Texas

Mom's Homemade Ice Cream

My mom, Marge Creech, has been a **Western Horseman** *subscriber for more than 50 years, and I love her recipe because there are no raw eggs!*

1 cup sugar

2 cans Eagle Brand condensed milk

2 tablespoons vanilla

12-ounce container Cool Whip

milk

Mix sugar, condensed milk, vanilla and Cool Whip. Pour creamy mixture into ice-cream maker.
Add milk to fill to the line on the creamer of a 1 ½-quart electric ice-cream maker, or about two-thirds full.
Freeze according to manufacturer's instructions.

Kami Peterson
Elizabeth, Colorado

Bread Pudding with Whiskey Sauce

Fill your kitchen with the sweet, rich, buttery aroma of old-fashioned bread pudding like grandma used to make.

Bread Pudding

2 eggs
2 tablespoons melted butter
2 tablespoons vanilla, Mexican if available
2½ cups milk
2 cups sugar
2 cups sourdough bread cut into 1-inch cubes
⅓ cup chopped pecans

Preheat oven to 325 degrees.

Beat the eggs, and add the butter, vanilla and milk. Gradually add the sugar and mix thoroughly until the sugar is dissolved.

Place bread cubes into the bottom of a 9-inch round baking dish.

Pour liquid over bread, making sure all the pieces are fully saturated. Sprinkle pecans over bread and push pecans down into the bread.

Bake in the oven 50 to 60 minutes. Serves 8 to 10.

Whiskey Sauce

½ cup sugar
1 stick butter
½ cup cream
¼ cup Jack Daniels

Combine the ingredients in a medium saucepan. Stir constantly over low heat until mixture reaches a low rolling boil.

Pour a small amount over individual servings of bread pudding.

Tom Perini
Buffalo Gap, Texas

From *Texas Cowboy Cooking* by Tom Perini, Comanche Moon Publishing and Perini Ranch, 2000.

JENNIFER DENISON

Grandma Spear's Dr Pepper Cake

Nothing satisfies your sweet tooth like an old family favorite with frosting.

Cake

1 cup butter

1 cup Dr Pepper

3 tablespoons cocoa

½ cup buttermilk

1 teaspoon baking soda

1 teaspoon vanilla extract

2 eggs

2 cups all-purpose flour

2 cups sugar

Preheat oven to 350 degrees.

Heat the butter, Dr Pepper and cocoa in a saucepan until boiling.
Remove from the heat and let cool.

In a mixing bowl, combine the buttermilk, baking soda, vanilla and eggs, mixing well.

In a separate bowl, combine the flour and sugar.

Then combine all three mixtures until blended. Pour the batter into a greased, 9-by-13-by-2-inch pan.

Bake for 20 to 25 minutes or until done. Test by inserting a toothpick at center of cake;
if the toothpick is free of crumbs, the cake is done.

When done, remove from the oven and pierce holes throughout the cake with a wooden skewer. Spread the
frosting on the cake and let cool.

Frosting

1 cup butter

3 tablespoons cocoa

6 tablespoons Dr Pepper

1½ cups sifted confectioners' sugar

While the cake bakes, prepare the frosting. Combine the butter, cocoa and Dr Pepper in a saucepan;
bring to a simmer. Whisk in the sugar and remove from heat.
Cool slightly before spreading on the warm cake, as described above.

Grady Spears,
Tolar, Texas

June Naylor
Fort Worth, Texas

From *Texas Cowboy Kitchen* by Grady Spears with June Naylor, Andrews McMeel Publishing, © 2007.

Cheryle's Peach Cobbler

Cobbler recipes are a dime a dozen, but this is a favorite on the Bar E Ranch Wagon.

2 1-pound cans of peaches
3 cans large crescent rolls
2 cups sugar
2 sticks unsalted butter
½ cup Sprite®
¼ teaspoon nutmeg
cinnamon to taste

If not cooking in a Dutch oven
over the coals,
preheat conventional oven to 350 degrees.

Drain the peaches and set aside
a small amount of fruit.

Spread out and separate the crescent
roll dough. Place peaches on the dough,
and roll up the crescent rolls.

Place the roll-ups in a seasoned 12-inch
Dutch oven rubbed with vegetable oil, or
a 9-by-13-inch baking dish coated with
cooking spray. Top with remaining peaches.

In a pan, melt butter and add sugar,
forming a thick syrup. Pour syrup and
Sprite over the cobbler, and sprinkle with
nutmeg and cinnamon.

Bake over coals until done,
or in a preheated 350-degree oven
for 35 to 40 minutes.

Tom, Cheryle, Jamie and Cody Elliott
Clinton, Arkansas

From the *Bar E Ranch Chuckwagon
Cookbook*, Bar E Ranch.

JENNIFER DENISON

135

Thanks to Western Horseman *Senior Editor Jennifer Denison, cowboy-style cooking continues to be a part of this outfit. Her horse, registered as Habanero Pepper, is also known as "Romeo."*

WALTER WORKMAN

Strawberry-Rhubarb Streusel

These delicate dessert tarts are bursting with a sweet, tangy filling and a dash of spice.

Streusel

4 tablespoons unsalted butter
⅓ cup pecan pieces
¼ cup light brown sugar
1 teaspoon ground cinnamon
½ teaspoon nutmeg
½ teaspoon ginger
½ teaspoon ground cloves
⅔ cup all-purpose flour

Filling

1½ cups diced rhubarb
1 cup diced strawberries
⅓ cup sugar
¼ cup all-purpose flour
1 teaspoon orange zest

Crust

4 ready-made pie crusts
1 beaten egg

Preheat oven to 375 degrees.

First, make the streusel by melting butter in a small pan over medium heat, stirring often. Remove butter from heat and add pecans, brown sugar and spices. Stir in flour until moist clumps form. Cover and chill.

Next, make the filling by combining all ingredients in a bowl and mixing well. Let filling stand until it looks moist, stirring occasionally.

Roll out piecrusts on a floured surface. Use cookie cutters to cut the top and bottom pieces of the tarts. Place tart bottoms on a greased cookie sheet. Spoon approximately 1 teaspoon of filling in the center of each tart and sprinkle a pinch of streusel over the filling. Then place tops on tarts. Crimp tart edges with a fork dampened with water to seal in filling and create a lace-like border. Brush beaten-egg wash over top of each tart.

Bake 15 to 18 minutes in preheated 375-degree oven. Cool tarts on rack for 30 minutes before serving. Sprinkle with colored sugar if desired. Makes approximately 15 tarts with 3-inch diameters.

Jennifer Denison
Sedalia, Colorado

JENNIFER DENISON

Cowboy Coffee Break

Fresh, hot coffee brewed over an open flame—the ultimate cowboy coffee-shop experience.
No barista in sight—just a cookie, coosie or cocinero keeping a watchful eye on the pot.

Long before there were corner cafés, cowboys sipped their java around an open campfire. Arbuckles' Ariosa Coffee, developed in 1865 by Pennsylvania entrepreneurs John Arbuckle and his brother, Charles, was considered the premium brew. The Starbucks brand of the day, Arbuckles' coffee beans were roasted, then coated with an egg and sugar glaze that preserved flavor and aroma. One-pound packages of the coffee, easily transported in crates, sold for 20 cents apiece.

Each bag contained a sweet surprise that was prized by the cowboys. A peppermint stick was hidden inside each bag of Arbuckles' coffee, much like the prize inside a box of Cracker Jacks. The cook often used the candy to bribe cowboys into grinding the coffee or performing other chores.

Cowboy coffee was brewed several ways over the campfire. One method was to keep adding grounds to the water "till a horseshoe floats." The other was to place the grounds in an old sock or cloth, tie the end of the sock in a knot to hold in the grounds, then place the sock in a pot of boiling water and allow the coffee to steep. This is the method Denney Willis, Arbuckles' owner, still prefers. He recommends adding 1 pound of coffee to 3 gallons of water.

Touted as the "coffee that won the West," Arbuckles' continues to be a staple on chuck-box shelves. To order Arbuckles' Ariosa Coffee in its original yellow packaging and with a peppermint inside, visit arbucklecoffee.com.

—Jennifer Denison

Six-Shooter Coffee, aka Bellywash

1½ pounds coffee
to 1 gallon water

Put coffee grounds into pot with a gallon of water and boil the hell out of it.

Do not worry about boiling too much for there is no such thing. Set it aside for a few minutes for the grounds to hit bottom before you pour.

Stella Hughes
Bacon & Beans

RECIPE INDEX

COOKBOOK CONTRIBUTORS

Jeannie Amen, Nampa, Idaho, always has loved horses. When she and her husband started their Green Springs Farm, they decided to breed horses for the temperament they preferred. Several years ago, she entered a *Western Horseman* recipe contest. As a result, her salad recipe, included here, has been featured in the magazine.

American Chuck Wagon Association, Brownfield, Texas, has proven a great resource for those interested in cowboy-style cooking. In fact, the Drunken Roast Beef recipe is adapted from the Circle F's recipe in *Second Helpings*, the ACWA cookbook. ACWA: 806-637-4272, info@ americanchuckwagon.org, or visit americanchuckwagon.org.

American Paint Horse Foundation, Fort Worth, Texas, primarily focuses on the heritage of the breed—both horses and people—and the education of Paint Horse youth, as well as biomedical equine health-care research. Linda Knowles' Sausage Stars recipe originally appeared in an APHF cookbook now out of print. Visit apha.com.

Jerry Baird, Snyder, Texas, has been instrumental in having the chuck wagon named the Official Vehicle of Texas and also helped establish the American Chuck Wagon Association. An award-winning chuck-wagon cook, Baird has his own line of gourmet seasonings and spices at jerrybairds.com. Contact him at 806-789-6098 or jerry@ snydertx.com.

Don Baskins, Tucumcari, N.M., author of the *Western Horseman* book *Well-Shod*, plied his trade through the years in western states, particularly along the Front Range of the Rockies. Magazine staffers soon learned that Don is as handy in the kitchen as he is at his forge, where he also enjoys making kitchen and grill utensils.

Bonnie Beers, Ontario, Ore., and daughter-in-law **Kimber Beers** first printed **Kate Mote**'s recipe for Rodeo Road Bars in their *Bring 'em on Home* cookbook, a tribute to their families and many others involved in professional rodeo. A portion of cookbook sales is donated to the Justin Cowboy Crisis Fund. Contact: bringemonhome@yahoo.com or bringemonhome.com.

Joncee Blake grew up helping in the family feed store in Weatherford, Texas, and now designs custom baby blankets and unique jewelry (montystudio.com.) She's as creative in her own way as her husband, western artist Teal Coke Blake (tealblake.com), Buckeye's son and a great-grandson of Samuel Coke Blake, a founding Quarter Horse breeder.

Jack and Karleen Boyd, Slaton, Texas, head up the award-winning Rocking K Chuck Wagon team and catering service. They have competed in chuck-wagon cook-offs for years, with their 2009 world-championship honors at the Lincoln County Cowboy Symposium in Ruidoso, N.M., a cherished win. Contact them at 806-549-3839.

Robert Boyd, Trent, Texas, is part of a large ranch-raised family. His mother, an excellent cook, believed that food presentation is an important part of well-planned meal. It's no surprise that Robert's catering service uses Old West and Southwestern themes particularly suited for those who enjoy the western lifestyle. Contact Robert at 325-660-5671.

Bobby and Teresa Bureleson, Weatherford, Texas, have a period-correct restored 1898 Mitchell wagon that they use in chuck-wagon cook-offs. In addition to being wagon cooks, Bobby builds custom spurs and bits, and Teresa is an award-winning cowgirl poet. Visit teresaburlesoncowgirlpoet.com.

Dalene Cameron, Bluff Dale, Texas, an Arizona native, is a driving force behind Craig Cameron's clinics, the Extreme Cowboy Race Association and Double Horn Ranch, which Craig appreciates. His horsemanship program is described in the *Western Horseman* books, *Ride Smart* and *Ride Smarter*. Contact: 800-274-0077 or craigcameron.com.

Jean Cates, Amarillo, Texas, and sister **Sue Cunningham**, Hartley, Texas, along with family members on the C Bar C wagon, have won numerous chuck-wagon cooking competitions. The National Cowgirl Hall of Fame inductees, who learned from father Dick Shepherd, have compiled three cookbooks: *Chuckwagon Recipes and Others*, *More Chuckwagon Recipes and Others*, and *Chuckwagon Recipes and Others No. 3*. Contact: 806-365-4596; ken-suec@xit.net.

Betty Cornforth, Caldwell, Idaho, has been reading *Western Horseman* since her high-school days and, at 84, still does—and she still enjoys being horseback, too. A huge rodeo fan who keeps up with all the sport's news, Betty eagerly anticipates her 85th celebration, which is planned during a special birthday trip to the National Finals Rodeo.

Suzie Newby Cox, Bloomfield, N.M., has won rodeo championships in American Junior Rodeo Association, Arizona High School Rodeo Association and Arizona Rodeo Association competition. Well-known in the ranching community, Suzie is married to artist Tim Cox, whose work is featured in *Western Horseman* magazines and books, and she runs their art-print and calendar business. Visit timcox.com.

Jacquelyn Deming, Fredericksburg, Texas, shares a Southwestern-inspired recipe that has graced the Deming family table for three generations. Her Chicken Mexicalli recipe, which originally appeared in *Western Horseman* magazine, came from an electrical bill insert in the 1960s and has been modified to suit the family's tastes.

Jennifer Denison, Sedalia, Colo., an award-winning journalist and senior editor for *Western Horseman*, has written two horse-handling and training books. She also packed through the Rockies with her folks, competed in youth and Little Britches rodeos, and learned her way around ranch work and cowboy-style meals. Contact: jennifer.denison@westernhorseman.com.

Darrell Dodds, Krum, Texas, a lifelong equine journalist and top photographer, retired as *Western Horseman* publisher in 2013, but continues to shoot great photographs for the western industry and now can spend more time horseback with wife Marty. Tamale-making, however, is a specialty. Contact: darrell_dodds@icloud.com

Cheryle and Tom Elliott, Clinton, Ark., serve fine meals from their Bar E Ranch wagon and also specialize in chuck-wagon cooking needs, from water barrels to tin ware to lid lifters—even the wagon itself. Find *The Bar E Ranch Chuckwagon Cookbook* and culinary supplies at cowboycooking.com, visit springfieldwagon.com, or call 800-959-5782.

Katie Frank, Fort Worth, Texas, an associate editor with *Western Horseman*, has a strong background in equine health care. At age 9, she first competed in 4-H and later showed in reining. Katie vied for all-around titles for several years on the American Quarter Horse Association circuit in the Pacific Northwest before ultimately moving to Texas. Contact: katie.frank@westernhorseman.com

Carol Laramore Gipson, Eaton, Colo., grew up in Wyoming with her brother, *Western Horseman*'s Butch Morgan. The lifelong horsewoman raised Quarter horses, a son, Scott, and a daughter, Tony, both rodeo competitors. Her husband Tom Gipson, who retired from steer tripping at 81, designed Chute Help automatic roping chutes. Contact: 855-248-8343, info@chutehelp.com or chutehelp.com.

Kit Haddock, Monument, Colo., has the Heart Bar Wagon, an 1890s Newton wagon that has been in service along the Front Range for more than 100 years. Haddock's wagon led Denver's 100th anniversary National Western Stock Show and Rodeo Parade. Contact the rancher and award-winning cook at kithaddock@mindspring.com.

Christine Hamilton, Fort Worth, Texas, editor of *Western Horseman* magazine, brings a strong stock-horse background and an eclectic recipe file to the outfit. Her mother's family is originally from South Georgia and her father's is from the West; Christine's recipes come from all points in between. Contact: chris.hamilton@westernhorseman.com.

Robert Heavirland, North Branch, Minn., won *Western Horseman*'s Dutch-oven recipe contest a few years back, but he's always quick to explain that his roast recipe was adapted from one the Circle F chuck wagon, Petersburg, Texas, had included in the American Chuck Wagon Association's *Second Helpings* cookbook. Contact: rheaviirland@yahoo.com

The Historical League, Tempe, Ariz., provided Rancho de la Osa's Margarita Pie and Pretzel Crust from the League's *Tastes & Treasures Cookbook, A Storytelling Cookbook of Historic Arizona*. Contact The Historical League: 480-929-0292, info@historicaleague.org or visit historicalleague.com.

Judy Engebretsen Howell, Morill, Neb., comes from a ranching family that used Quarter Horses for ranch work, as well as for the children to show. Because her dad bought calves in southern Colorado and New Mexico, Judy's first taste of Mexican Vermicelli was in a New Mexico ranch cookhouse in the 1960s. Her husband suggested that she send the recipe to *Western Horseman*.

Nancy Hughes, customer-service representative for Cowboy Publishing Group, shares not only her own recipes, but also one from her mother **Sally Morris**. Nancy is known as the Martha Stewart in the Fort Worth offices shared by *Barrel Horse News, Western Horseman* and *Quarter Horse News*, all part of Morris Communications. Contact: nancy.hughes@cowboypublishing.com.

Stella Hughes might be gone, but she's never forgotten. The popular, longtime *Western Horseman* "Bacon & Beans" columnist also wrote the cookbook by that same name, among others. In fact, Stella received a Western Writers of America Spur Award for best nonfiction Western—*Hashknife Cowboy: Recollections of Mack Hughes*—in which she wrote about her late husband's experiences.

Dirk Kempthorne of Sun Valley, former Governor of Idaho, U.S. Senator and Secretary of the Department of the Interior, obviously has been no stranger to flavorful western meals. Idaho's Bean & Pasta Salad, his recipe from Boots Reynolds' *Boots 'n' Beans* has been reprinted here courtesy of the Reynolds family and Keokee Company Publishing.

Barbara Kennedy, Desert Hills, Ariz., has competed in chuck-wagon cook-offs for about 15 years, and the award-winning Cowgirls Forever team uses a restored 1880s wagon. Barbara not only shares her Chili Verde recipe, but also the Chapter 4 tips for campfire cooking. Contact: cowgirlsforevercamp@hotmail.com or cowgirlsforever.org.

Madge King, Jackson, Miss., is known for the fine southern-style dishes she serves, and seats at her table are always in demand. Her son, *Western Horseman* General Manager Ernie King, has proclaimed her "the best cook in the world." She shares two of Ernie's favorites—chocolate pie and oatmeal cookies. Contact: ernie.king@westernhorseman.com.

141

Linda Knowles, Fort Worth, Texas, is show-approval manager for the American Paint Horse Association. She previously had contributed her Sausage Stars recipe to a cookbook, now out of print, benefiting the American Paint Horse Foundation's work with young people in the horse industry and with equine research. Visit apha.com.

Deanna Lally, Snohomish, Wash., a reining-horse trainer and coach, is a talented western artist and author of two *Western Horseman* books: *The Art of Hackamore Training with Al Dunning and Benny Guitron* and the soon-to-be released *Down the Fence*, also written with Al Dunning. For more information, visit dlallyperformancehorses.com.

Becky Prunty Lisle, Charleston, Nev., continues a five-generation tradition, working horseback on the family ranch in northern Elko County. Although ranch life rarely is as neatly packaged as the Bierocks made from her recipe, it's the lifestyle she prefers. The family breeds, trains and sells ranch Quarter horses. Learn more at pruntyhorses.com.

Marianne McCartney, Throckmorton, Texas, and husband Todd have deep roots in the ranching industry, particularly with the R.A. Brown Ranch and the fine Quarter Horses and cattle raised there, which have been featured in *Western Horseman*. Todd also narrated the audio version of *Legends, Volume 1*. Contact: rabrownranch.com or cowboytalent.com.

Kathy McCraine, Prescott, Ariz., celebrates the Southwest's ranching lifestyle with her fine writing and photographs in her book *Cow Country Cooking*, in which Indian Fry Bread and her mother-in-law's slaw recipes originally appeared. Given her ranching background, Kathy's photographs and writing also have been featured in *Western Horseman* magazine and the outfit's *Legendary Ranches* book. Contact: kathymccraine.com.

Cynthia McFarland, Williston, Fla., a longtime contributor to *Western Horseman*, has written *Cow-Horse Confidence with Martin Black* and *Ride the Journey with Chris Cox*, as well as *The Horseman's Guide to Tack and Equipment*. Equally knowledgeable about the Thoroughbred industry, Cynthia writes for national equine publications and covers food, health and lifestyle topics for regional Florida publications. Contact her at 352-528-1259 or yumasierra@aol.com.

Charlene and Butch Morgan, Elbert, Colo., have been with *Western Horseman* for years, representing the outfit at equine trade shows and events nationwide. They submitted several favorite recipes and properly credited their sources—Butch's sister, **Carol Laramore Gipson**, and **Pat Honey Mosher**, whose daughter, Renee, is married to the Morgans' son, C.L. Contact: butch.morgan@westernhorseman.com.

Susan Morrison, Fort Worth, Texas, is an award-winning equine journalist and avid cutting-horse enthusiast and competitor. She's also *Western Horseman*'s managing editor and author of Craig Cameron's latest book, *Ride Smarter*. Prior to joining the magazine staff, Susan had been with *Quarter Horse News*, a sister publication that is also part of Morris Communications' Cowboy Publishing Group. Contact susan.morrison@westernhorseman.com

Pat Honey Mosher, La Junta, Colo., has had nice ranch-raised horses for sale through the years and has been a Quarter Horse breeder since 1980—and for good reason. Her kids all rodeoed, including Renee, daughter-in-law to Butch and Charlene Morgan, who submitted Pat's Macaroni and Macaroni and Corn Casserole recipe for this cookbook.

Kate Mote, Culver, Ore., wife of world-champion bareback rider Bobby Mote, made Rodeo Road Bars while traveling the circuit and shared the recipe in Bonnie and Kimber Beers' *Bring 'em on Home* cookbook. A portion of the book sales at bringemonhome.com is donated to the Justin Cowboy Crisis Fund.

June Naylor, Fort Worth, Texas, learned to ride at age 8 and has loved riding ever since, mostly Western-style nationwide, but also in Hawaii and Ireland. Living near the Will Rogers Memorial Complex gives her the opportunity to enjoy varied horse events year-round. She has co-authored cookbooks with chuck-wagon cook Grady Spears. Contact: june@junenaylor.com.

Clyde Nelson, Clarke, Colo., executive chef at The Home Ranch, is "allergic to cities." That's a great thing for those enjoying his fine Rocky Mountain cuisine, as well as Home Ranch experiences, such as the combination riding and yoga retreat with horsewoman Tammy Pate and yogini Janice Baxter. For information and more recipes, visit homeranch.com.

Linda Parelli, Pagosa Springs, Colo., and husband Pat spearhead the Parelli Natural Horsemanship team that serves riders both here and abroad. Since Linda, a dressage rider, met Pat, she has made chronicling PNH techniques her mission. Contact PNH at 800-642-3335 or pnhusa@parelli.com, or visit parelli.com.

Tom Perini, Buffalo Gap, Texas, serves his award-winning bread pudding recipe, featured in the magazine and included here, as a signature dish at his Perini Ranch Steakhouse, also in Buffalo Gap. The recipe originally appeared in the restaurateur's cookbook, *Texas Cowboy Cooking*, available at periniranch.com or by calling 800-367-1721.

Kami Peterson, Franktown, Colo., a senior account manager, joined *Western Horseman*'s sales department in 2002. She and husband Daren divide their time between Colorado and Arizona, producing team-roping events in both states, and are partners in Ullman-Peterson Events LLC and the Bob Feist Invitational. Contact: kami.peterson@westernhorseman.com.

Boots Reynolds' entertaining artwork has been featured in *Western Horseman* for years. Dick Spencer, longtime magazine publisher, and Boots, both now deceased, loved cartooning and anything comical. Becky Reynolds is "sure they are both up there tellin' stories and drawin' funny 'pitchers' and having a great time!" Keokee Co. published *Boots 'n' Beans* in 2008.

Kent Rollins, Hollis, Okla., is an award-winning chuck-wagon cook and longtime contributor to *Western Horseman*'s cooking column, and he has made numerous television appearances promoting cowboy-style cooking. Kent and his wife, Shannon, hold Red River Chuck Wagon Cooking Schools annually and have a line of Red River Ranch products, including seasonings at kentrollins.com.

Ryan Sankey, Roberts, Mont., is a true woman of the West; she has real enthusiasm for good cooking, as well as for rodeo rough-stock. The daughter of stock contractor Ike Sankey of Joliet, Mont., Ryan is a partner with her parents and her brother, Wade, in Sankey Pro Rodeo. To learn more, visit sankeyprorodeo.com.

Fran Devereux Smith, Fort Worth, Texas, an award-winning journalist with *Western Horseman* for 20-plus years, was managing editor prior to working primarily on books for the outfit. She has written several, including *First Horse*, *Ranch Horsemanship* with Curt Pate, *Team Roping with Jake and Clay*, and *Ranch-Horse Versatility* with Mike Major. Contact: fran.smith@westernhorseman.com.

Grady Spears, Tolar, Texas, co-wrote *The Texas Cowboy Kitchen* with June Naylor of Fort Worth, Texas, a cookbook that includes his grandmother's Dr Pepper cake recipe, which previously has been featured in *Western Horseman*. The cookbook, *The Texas Cowboy Kitchen*, from Andrews McMeel Publishing, is available at major booksellers, as are other Spears cookbooks.

Joe St. Clair, a chuck-wagon cook in Arizona previously shared his Indian Fry Bread recipe with Kathy McCraine for her *Cow Country Cooking*, which provides great recipes and entertaining insights about the state's ranching industry and some of its characters. She, in turn, has shared Joe's recipe with our readers. Find the cookbook at kathymccraine.com.

St. Mary's Catholic Church, Graham, Texas, created *Cooking with St. Mary's* in 1995, which found a place on Marianne McCartney's kitchen bookshelf, given her ties to the parish. Although the cookbook is no longer in print, the Mandarin Orange Salad recipe from the church cookbook continues to find a place at the McCartney table.

Jeff Tracey, Oregon City, Ore., is a lifelong horseman and an approved judge in several equine associations. He also has years of radio and television broadcasting experience, which he enthusiastically uses to gain followers for the Western lifestyle and cooking the cowboy way. Visit thecowboycook.com.

University of Arizona Press in Tucson, which first published *Chuck Wagon Cookin'* by Stella Hughes in 1974, has allowed us to reprint Stella's recipe for Humpy's Fried Cornmeal Bread. "Humpy," who had been a cook on the Hashknife outfit in Winslow, Ariz., had given the recipe to Stella years ago. Contact: uapress.arizona.edu.

Rex and Sheryl Wailes, Bennett, Colo., use their 1896 Bain wagon, the Lizzie II, for catering, brandings and chuck-wagon cook-offs. The chuck box is made from the sides of a Wailes family grain wagon; toolbox and boot box are made from old grain bins. The Lizzie II wagon has won awards at cook-offs in Arizona, Colorado and New Mexico. Contact: lostcreek@esrta.com.

Tina and Daryl Waite, Hugo, Colo., manage the Withers Ranch and have restored their own working wagon, primarily to feed spring branding crews at the ranch or on neighboring outfits. The wagon also represents Withers Ranch at chuck-wagon cook-offs. The Waites are strong ranch rodeo supporters. Contact twaite@esrta.com.

Tonya Ward, Weatherford, Texas, has worked with *Western Horseman* advertising representatives and their clientele for many years. In her spare time the lifelong horsewoman and reining enthusiast manages trade shows at such events as the Red Steagall Cowboy Gathering and Windy Ryon Memorial Roping.

Bonnie Welch, Wolfforth, Texas, and Fowler, Colo., and **Deanna White**, Kiowa, Colo., both in the cattle business, created *Kitchen Keepsakes by Request* in 1993, from which Marianne McCartney submitted the Avocado Tossed Salad recipe. Three Keepsakes cookbooks are available at Amazon.com, or call 303-621-2802 or 806-789-7276.

January and Cory Wiese, Dripping Springs, Texas, are no strangers to good cooking. Cory, *Western Horseman*'s digital media manager, is son of Linda and Ted Wiese, whose Cowboy Bistro serves rodeo contestants. January has worked as a winery consultant and wine-event coordinator. Contact: cory.wiese@westernhorseman.com.

Linda and Ted Wiese, Payette, Idaho, began a local ministry in 1986 at a rodeo practice pen for high-school and college competitors. Now Rockin W Rodeo Ministries serves professional rodeo contestants' spiritual needs, and the couple's mobile kitchen, The Cowboy Bistro, also feeds them at major events. Contact: 208-890-5894; cowboybistro.com.

Patricia Wilson, Topeka, Kan., is aunt to *Western Horseman* Senior Editor Jennifer Denison. The two must be kindred spirits when it comes to hearth, home—and kitchen. Several of Pat's recipes are included, and perhaps the most unique is Fruit Salsa with Cinnamon and Sugar Tortilla Chips.

Marsha Witte, Peyton, Colo., ranch-raised near Steamboat Springs, Colo., is a top breeder of Texas Longhorn Cattle. Randy, her husband of 44 years, retired as *Western Horseman* publisher after 29 years with the outfit. Marsha's sweet potato recipe came from the late **Melitta Bergen**, whose husband, Chan, retired as *Western Horseman* editor after 25 years with the magazine, which followed his 21-year career in the United States Army. Contact randymarshawitte@aol.com.

Women for Abilene Christian University published *Tasteful Traditions* in which the recipe for Chicken and Green Chilies Casserole originally appeared, as submitted by Boots Hill, a longtime ACU supporter. Longtime *Western Horseman* staffer Tonya Ward, an Abilene native and former ACU student, in turn, passed along the recipe for inclusion here.

PROFILE
JENNIFER DENISON

WALTER WORKMAN

Colorado native Jennifer Denison grew up riding horses, hunting, camping and cooking over an open fire in the Rocky Mountains. She started riding in her local 4-H club and the National Little Britches Rodeo Association. In college, she continued to run barrels, but gradually returned to her backcountry roots, riding with her father, Lew, an avid hunter and packer.

Even though she preferred to be outdoors with horses, Jennifer also spent time in the kitchen, helping her mom prepare family meals, baking cookies for special occasions and later mastering meal-time recipes. Some of her family's favorites are found in this book.

Jennifer, an American Horse Publications Student Award winner, graduated from Colorado State University in 1995 with a double-major in Equine Science and Technical Journalism. She soon began her equine journalism career, spending six years developing her writing and photography skills and knowledge of the performance-horse industry before coming to *Western Horseman* in 2002. Currently the magazine's senior editor, she has written hundreds of articles about horsemanship, ranching and the Western lifestyle, some earning American Horse Publications awards.

She is also the co-author of two training books: *John Lyons' Bringing Up Baby* (2002, Trafalgar Square Publishing), and *Backcountry Basics* (2009, Western Horseman Books) with Mike Kinsey.

Western Horseman, which focuses on all facets of the stock-horse industry, including the Western lifestyle, has been a perfect fit for Jennifer. As cowboy culture editor, she truly appreciates Western art, craftsmanship and cowboy-style cooking, and has developed magazine sections devoted to these topics. She has interviewed and worked with such noted contemporary chuck-wagon and cowboy cooks as Sue Cunningham and Jean Cates, Tom Perini, Kent Rollins and Grady Spears.

Jennifer enjoys creatively preparing and styling meals for family gatherings, barn parties, brandings and get-togethers with friends. Each fall, she hosts an old-fashioned harvest party at her home to give friends and family a taste of Dutch-oven cooking and country life, including horseback rides for the kids. Cooking, to Jennifer, is more than preparing food, it's about bringing people together and sharing a taste of her lifestyle.